THE CITY O[
THE ULTIMA[

BOSTON

TRAVEL GUIDE

DIANA L.
MITCHELL

© **Copyright 2024 - All rights reserved.**

The content contained within this book may not be reproduced, duplicated or transmitted without direct written permission from the author or the publisher.

Under no circumstances will any blame or legal responsibility be held against the publisher, or author, for any damages, reparation, or monetary loss due to the information contained within this book, either directly or indirectly.

Legal Notice:

This book is copyright protected. It is only for personal use. You cannot amend, distribute, sell, use, quote or paraphrase any part, or the content within this book, without the consent of the author or publisher.

Disclaimer Notice:

Please note the information contained within this document is for educational and entertainment purposes only. All effort has been executed to present accurate, up to date, reliable, complete information. No warranties of any kind are declared or implied. Readers acknowledge that the author is not engaged in the rendering of legal, financial, medical or professional advice. The content within this book has been derived from various sources. Please consult a licensed professional before attempting any techniques outlined in this book.

By reading this document, the reader agrees that under no circumstances is the author responsible for any losses, direct or indirect, that are incurred as a result of the use of the information contained within this document, including, but not limited to, errors, omissions, or inaccuracies.

Cover image: © Lunamarina via canva.com

Dear reader, thanks a lot for purchasing my book.

To help you plan your trip even more efficiently, I have included an interactive map powered by Google My Maps.

To access it, scan the QR code below.

Happy travelling!

A Note to Our Valued Readers

Thank you for choosing this travel guide as your companion for exploring the world.

I want to take a moment to address a concern you might have regarding the absence of photographs in this book.

As an independent author and publisher, I strive to deliver high-quality, informative content at an affordable price.

Including photographs in a printed book, however, presents significant challenges. Licensing high-quality images can be extremely costly, and unfortunately, I have no control over the print quality of images within the book.

Because these guides are printed and shipped by Amazon, I am unable to review the final print quality before they reach your hands.

So, rather than risk compromising your reading experience with subpar visuals, I've chosen to focus on providing detailed, insightful content that will help you make the most of your travels.

While this guide may not contain photos, it's packed with valuable information, insider tips, and recommendations to ensure you have an enriching and memorable journey.

Additionally, there's an interactive map powered by Google My Maps—an essential tool to help you plan your trip.

I encourage you to supplement your reading with online resources where you can find up-to-date images and visuals of the destinations covered in this guide.

I hope you find this book a helpful and inspiring resource as you embark on your next adventure.

Thank you for your understanding and support.

Safe travels,

Diana

Table of Contents

Welcome to Boston 1
   Why visit Boston? 1
      Iconic Landmarks 2
      Cultural Diversity 2
      World-Class Museums and Art Art 2
      Theater and Entertainment 2
      Culinary Delights 3
      Shopping Mecca 3
      Green Spaces and Recreation 3
      Historical Significance 3
      Vibrant Neighborhoods 3
      Year-Round Attractions 4

Getting Around 5
   Public Transportation 5
      Subway System 5
      Bus Routes 6
      Boston Harbor Ferry 8
   Taxis and Rideshares 9
      Traditional Taxis 9
      Uber and Lyft 10
   Biking 12
      Bluebikes Program 12

What to See and Do 15
   Iconic Landmarks 15
      Boston Common 15
      Faneuil Hall 16
      Quincy Market 16

Paul Revere House 17
Old North Church 18
Massachusetts State House 19
Boston Public Garden 20
Bunker Hill Monument 21
USS Constitution 22
Fenway Park 23
New England Aquarium 24
Boston Tea Party Ships & Museum 25
John Hancock Tower 26
Boston Public Library 27
Arnold Arboretum 27
The Boston Harbor Islands National and State Park 28

Museums and Cultural Institutions 31
Museum of Fine Arts, Boston 31
Isabella Stewart Gardner Museum 32
Boston Children's Museum 33
Museum of Science 34
Harvard Museum of Natural History 35
MIT Museum 36
John F. Kennedy Presidential Library and Museum 37
Boston African American National Historic Site 38
Institute of Contemporary Art 39
Nichols House Museum 41

Theaters and Performances 43
Boston Opera House 43
Wang Theatre 44
Orpheum Theatre 45

    Cutler Majestic Theatre 46

    Emerson Colonial Theatre 46

    Wilbur Theatre 47

    Boston Symphony Hall 48

    Charles Playhouse 49

    Huntington Theatre 50

    Shubert Theatre 51

Historic Sites 53

    Freedom Trail 53

    Old State House 54

    Old South Meeting House 55

    King's Chapel 56

    Granary Burying Ground 56

    Boston Massacre Site 57

    Fort Warren (Boston Harbor Islands) 58

    Dorchester Heights 59

    Plimoth Plantation (near Boston) 60

    Minute Man National Historical Park (near Boston) 61

Observation Decks 63

    Skywalk Observatory at the Prudential Center 63

    Custom House Tower Observation Deck 63

Neighborhood Exploration 65

    Beacon Hill 65

    North End (Little Italy) 66

    Back Bay 67

    South End 68

    Cambridge (Harvard Square) 69

    Seaport District 70

- Charlestown ... 71
- Jamaica Plain ... 72
- South Boston (Southie) ... 73
- Allston-Brighton ... 74
- Roslindale ... 75
- Chinatown ... 76

Food and Dining ... 79

Iconic Boston Foods ... 79
- Clam Chowder ... 79
- Lobster Rolls ... 79
- Baked Beans ... 80

Fine Dining ... 81
- Award-Winning Restaurants ... 81
- Internationally Inspired Fine Dining ... 81

Casual Eateries ... 82
- Neighborhood Favorites ... 82
- Trendy Cafes and Diners ... 83

Street Food and Food Trucks ... 83
- Classic Street Food ... 84
- Gourmet Food Trucks ... 84
- Pop-Up Markets ... 84

Ethnic Cuisine ... 85
- North End ... 85
- Chinatown ... 86

Food Markets ... 86
- Quincy Market ... 87
- Boston Public Market ... 87
- SoWa Open Market ... 88

Welcome to Boston

Welcome to Boston, a historic and vibrant metropolis known as the "City on a Hill." Bursting with energy and rich in cultural heritage, Boston is a city of firsts, making it one of the most dynamic cities in the United States. Whether you're a first-time visitor or a seasoned traveler, the city's iconic skyline, diverse neighborhoods, and rich history offer endless opportunities for exploration and adventure.

Boston is composed of numerous distinct neighborhoods—each with its unique character and charm. From the historic charm of Beacon Hill to the academic atmosphere of Cambridge, the multicultural vibrancy of Dorchester, the artistic enclaves of Jamaica Plain, and the bustling energy of the Seaport District, there's something for everyone in Boston.

The city is home to some of the world's most famous landmarks, such as the Freedom Trail, Fenway Park, and the Boston Common. It's a global hub for education, culture, and innovation, boasting world-class museums, theaters, and music venues. Whether you're strolling through the Boston Public Garden, catching a Red Sox game, exploring historic sites, or savoring culinary delights from around the globe, Boston promises an unforgettable experience.

Join us as we guide you through the best of what Boston has to offer, providing tips and insights to help you make the most of your visit to this extraordinary city.

Why visit Boston?

Boston is a destination like no other, offering a unique blend of history, culture, and modernity that captivates millions of visitors each year. Here are some compelling reasons why Boston should be at the top of your travel list:

Iconic Landmarks

Boston is home to some of the nation's most recognizable landmarks. From the historic Freedom Trail, which tells the story of America's founding, to the iconic Fenway Park, the oldest ballpark in Major League Baseball, these sites are must-sees for any visitor.

Cultural Diversity

Boston is a true melting pot, with a rich tapestry of cultures and communities. This diversity is reflected in the city's neighborhoods, festivals, and culinary scene, offering a global experience within the city's historic framework.

World-Class Museums and Art Art

enthusiasts will find paradise in Boston, with its array of world-renowned museums and galleries. The Museum of Fine Arts, the Isabella Stewart Gardner Museum, and the Institute of Contemporary Art showcase masterpieces from around the world, while countless smaller galleries and cultural institutions offer a deeper dive into various art forms and historical periods.

Theater and Entertainment

Theater lovers flock to Boston for its vibrant performing arts scene. With an array of shows, from classic plays to cutting-edge performances, there's always something new and exciting to see. Beyond the theater, the city's comedy clubs, live music venues, and performance spaces ensure endless entertainment options.

Culinary Delights

Boston's food scene is legendary, offering everything from Michelin-starred fine dining to iconic street food. Indulge in fresh seafood at the historic Quincy Market, savor international cuisines in diverse neighborhoods, or explore food markets like Boston Public Market for a true culinary adventure.

Shopping Mecca

Boston is a shopper's paradise, featuring luxury boutiques on Newbury Street, trendy shops in the South End, and unique finds in street markets. Whether you're looking for high-end fashion, vintage treasures, or quirky souvenirs, the city has it all.

Green Spaces and Recreation

Amidst the urban hustle, Boston boasts beautiful parks and green spaces. Boston Common offers a serene escape with its historic grounds and walking trails, while smaller parks like the Rose Kennedy Greenway provide unique urban oases.

Historical Significance

With its rich history, Boston offers numerous sites of historical importance. Explore the Boston Tea Party Ships and Museum and the Paul Revere House to gain insights into the city's past and its role in shaping modern America.

Vibrant Neighborhoods

Each Boston neighborhood has its distinct character and charm. From the historic cobblestone streets of the North End and the upscale allure of

Back Bay to the hipster haven of Jamaica Plain and the academic stronghold of Cambridge, there's always a new area to discover.

Year-Round Attractions

No matter the season, Boston offers a plethora of activities and events. Enjoy summer concerts in the park, fall foliage along the Charles River, winter ice skating at Frog Pond, and spring blooms at the Arnold Arboretum.

Boston's dynamic spirit, cultural depth, and endless possibilities make it an unforgettable destination for travelers from around the world. Whether you're here for a weekend or an extended stay, Boston promises experiences that will leave you wanting to return time and again.

Getting Around

Public Transportation

Boston boasts an extensive and efficient public transportation system, making it easy to navigate the city without a car. Here's an overview of the key public transportation options, including the subway system, bus routes, and the ferry services.

Subway System

Overview:

- The MBTA subway system, commonly known as the "T," is one of the oldest public transit systems in the United States, with over 145 stations across Boston and surrounding areas.
- Operated by the Massachusetts Bay Transportation Authority (MBTA), the subway provides a convenient and reliable mode of transportation for millions of residents and visitors.

Subway Lines:

The subway system consists of four primary lines, each identified by a color:

- Red Line: Serves areas including Cambridge, downtown Boston, and Ashmont/Braintree.
- Orange Line: Runs from Oak Grove in Malden to Forest Hills in Jamaica Plain.
- Blue Line: Connects Wonderland in Revere to Bowdoin in downtown Boston.
- Green Line: Divided into four branches (B, C, D, E), serving areas from downtown Boston to Brookline, Newton, and Medford. • Trains typically run local, stopping at every station along their route.

Using the Subway:

- CharlieCard: The standard fare payment method. Purchase and reload at station vending machines or retail locations. Offers discounted fares compared to paper tickets.
- CharlieTicket: A paper ticket that can be used for single or multiple rides. Available at vending machines.
- Contactless Payment: The MBTA is rolling out contactless payment options, allowing users to tap their contactless card or device at the turnstile to pay.
- Maps and Apps: Subway maps are available in stations and online. Apps like MBTA Tracker and Transit provide real-time updates and route planning.
- Safety Tips: Stay aware of your surroundings, avoid empty cars, and keep belongings secure. Use staffed entrances and exits, especially late at night.

Key Stations:

- South Station: Major transfer point for the Red Line, Amtrak, and MBTA Commuter Rail.
- North Station: Connects the Green and Orange Lines with Amtrak and MBTA Commuter Rail. Park Street: Central hub connecting the Red and Green Lines.
- Downtown Crossing: Connects the Red and Orange Lines, with access to shopping areas.
- Government Center: Connects the Green and Blue Lines, near City Hall and Faneuil Hall.

Bus Routes

Overview:

- Boston's public transportation system, managed by the Massachusetts Bay Transportation Authority (MBTA), complements the subway (the "T") by providing bus services that reach areas not well-served by trains. Buses operate throughout the Greater Boston area, with numerous routes, including local, express, and Silver Line services.

Types of Buses:

- **Local Buses**: Make frequent stops, serving specific neighborhoods and routes.
- **Express Buses**: Provide faster service with fewer stops, primarily catering to commuters traveling between suburbs and downtown Boston.
- **Silver Line**: Offers faster service with dedicated bus lanes, fewer stops, and off-board fare payment. It includes routes that serve Logan Airport and the Seaport District.

Using the Bus:

- **CharlieCard/CharlieTicket/Mobile Payment**: These fare payment methods are the same as for the subway. CharlieCards can be tapped on the farebox, and mobile payment users can scan their devices.
- **Bus Stops**: Look for green and white signs with route numbers. Check schedules and maps posted at stops or use transit apps for real-time information.
- **Boarding**: Enter through the front door and exit through the rear door (except on Silver Line, where all doors can be used for boarding and exiting).

Popular Routes:

- **Route 1**: Connects Harvard Square in Cambridge to Dudley Station in Roxbury, traveling through Central Square and Massachusetts Avenue.
- **Route 66**: Runs from Harvard Square in Cambridge to Nubian Square in Roxbury, serving Allston and Brookline.
- **Route 39**: Connects Forest Hills Station in Jamaica Plain to Back Bay Station, traveling along Huntington Avenue.
- **Silver Line SL1**: Provides rapid transit from South Station to Logan Airport, serving the Seaport District.

Boston Harbor Ferry

Overview:

The Boston Harbor Ferry provides vital links between various parts of the city and surrounding areas, including Charlestown, East Boston, and the Seaport District. It operates multiple routes and offers scenic and convenient travel options.

Route and Schedule:

- **Routes**: The ferry routes include services from Long Wharf to Charlestown Navy Yard, East Boston, and other destinations.
- **Schedule**: Ferries run frequently during peak hours and less frequently during off-peak hours. Check the MBTA website for exact times.

Experience:

- **Scenic Views**: Enjoy stunning views of the Boston skyline, the Boston Harbor Islands, and historic landmarks.
- **Amenities**: Terminals offer various amenities, including food and beverage options, restrooms, and waiting areas.
- **Accessibility**: Both terminals and ferries are fully accessible for passengers with disabilities.

Connecting Transportation:

- **Long Wharf**: Access to multiple subway lines (Blue, Orange), buses, and commuter rail services.
- **Charlestown Navy Yard**: Connections to bus routes and the nearby Bunker Hill community.
- **Seaport District**: Connections to Silver Line buses and access to the vibrant Seaport area.

Boston's public transportation system is extensive and user-friendly, making it easy to get around the city efficiently. Whether you're taking the subway, riding the bus, or enjoying a scenic trip on the Boston Harbor Ferry, you'll find a range of options to suit your travel needs.

Taxis and Rideshares

Boston offers a variety of taxi and rideshare options that provide convenient and flexible transportation throughout the city and its surrounding areas. Here's a detailed look at Boston's traditional taxis, Uber, and Lyft, including how to use them, fare information, and tips for a smooth ride.

Traditional Taxis

Overview:
- Boston's traditional taxis are regulated by the Boston Police Department's Hackney Carriage Unit.
- They can be hailed on the street, found at taxi stands throughout the city, or booked by phone.

How to Hail a Taxi:
- **Street Hailing:** Stand on the curb and raise your arm when you see an available cab. An available cab's roof light will be illuminated.
- **Taxi Stands:** Often located near major hotels, transportation hubs, and popular attractions.
- **Telephone Dispatch:** Many taxi companies in Boston offer phone dispatch services, making it convenient to book a ride in advance.

Fare Information:
- **Base Fare:** Starts at $2.60, with additional charges based on distance and time.
- **Surcharges:** Additional charges may apply during peak times or for extra services like luggage handling.
- **Tolls:** Any bridge or tunnel tolls are added to the fare.
- **Tips:** A customary tip for taxi drivers is 15-20% of the total fare.
- **Payment:** Accepted in cash and credit/debit cards. All cabs are equipped with card readers.

Tips for a Smooth Ride:

- **Provide Clear Directions:** Have your destination address ready and communicate it clearly to the driver.
- **Safety:** Make sure the taxi's medallion number and driver's information are displayed on the dashboard.
- **Receipt:** Always ask for a receipt at the end of your ride for record-keeping or in case you need to retrieve lost items.

Uber and Lyft

Overview:
- Uber and Lyft are popular rideshare services in Boston, offering convenient, app-based transportation options.
- These services provide a range of vehicle types, from budget-friendly rides to luxury options.

Using Uber and Lyft:
- **Download the App:** Available on both iOS and Android platforms.
- **Create an Account:** Sign up with your email, phone number, and payment information.
- **Request a Ride:** Enter your destination and choose the type of ride (e.g., UberX, UberPOOL, Lyft, Lyft XL).
- **Track Your Ride:** The app provides real-time tracking of your driver's location and estimated arrival time.
- **Payment:** Automatically charged to your registered payment method. Tips can be added through the app.

Fare Information:
- **Base Fare:** Varies by service type and time of day.
- **Surge Pricing:** During peak times or high demand, prices may increase due to surge pricing.
- **Tolls:** Any applicable bridge or tunnel tolls are added to the fare.
- **Tips:** Tipping is optional but appreciated and can be done through the app.

Service Options:
- **UberX/Lyft:** Standard ride for up to four passengers.
- **UberPOOL/Lyft Shared:** Shared rides with other passengers heading in the same direction, offering a lower fare.

- **UberXL/Lyft XL:** Larger vehicles for groups up to six passengers.
- **Uber Black/Lyft Lux:** Premium black car service for a more luxurious ride experience.

Tips for a Smooth Ride:
- **Confirm Your Ride:** Verify the driver's name, vehicle make, model, and license plate before getting in.
- **Safety Features:** Both apps offer safety features such as sharing your trip status with friends and family and in-app emergency assistance.
- **Pickup Locations:** Choose a safe and convenient pickup location, especially in busy areas.
- **Ratings:** Rate your driver after the ride to provide feedback on your experience.

Comparisons and Considerations
- **Availability:** Traditional taxis are typically more abundant in high-traffic areas like Downtown Boston, while rideshare services can be more convenient in suburban areas or less busy neighborhoods.
- **Cost:** Rideshare fares can be more variable due to surge pricing, whereas traditional taxi fares are more consistent but may include surcharges during peak times.
- **Convenience:** Rideshare apps offer the convenience of cashless payment and real-time tracking, while traditional taxis can be easily hailed on the street without the need for an app.

Whether you choose the traditional taxi or a modern rideshare service like Uber or Lyft, Boston provides a range of options to suit your transportation needs. Understanding how to use these services effectively can help you navigate the city with ease and make the most of your time in Boston.

Biking

Bluebikes Program

Overview:
- Bluebikes is Boston's bike-sharing system, offering a convenient and eco-friendly way to get around the city.
- Launched in 2011, it has expanded to include thousands of bikes and hundreds of stations across Boston, Cambridge, Somerville, and Brookline.

How Bluebikes Works:
- **Membership Options:** Choose from various membership plans, including Single Trip, Adventure Pass, and Annual Membership.
  - **Single Trip:** Best for occasional users, allows a 30-minute ride for a fixed fee.
  - **Adventure Pass:** Ideal for tourists, offers unlimited 2-hour rides in a 24-hour period.
  - **Annual Membership:** Best for residents, includes unlimited 45-minute rides for a year.
- **Finding a Bike:** Use the Bluebikes app or website to locate nearby stations and check bike availability.
- **Unlocking a Bike:** Use the app, your Bluebikes key (for annual members), or a ride code to unlock a bike at any station.
- **Riding and Returning:** Enjoy your ride and return the bike to any Bluebikes station. Make sure the bike is securely docked to end your ride.

Benefits of Using Bluebikes:
- **Flexibility:** Easily navigate through traffic and access areas not well-served by public transportation.
- **Health and Fitness:** Enjoy a workout while commuting or sightseeing.
- **Environmentally Friendly:** Reduce your carbon footprint by opting for a bike over a car or taxi.

Tips for a Smooth Ride:
- **Plan Your Route:** Use the Bluebikes app to plan safe and efficient routes.

- **Follow Traffic Rules:** Obey all traffic signals and signs, use bike lanes where available, and signal your turns.
- **Safety Gear:** Always wear a helmet and consider using reflective clothing or lights, especially at night.
- **Station Availability:** Check the app for docking station availability near your destination to avoid last-minute hassles.

Popular Routes and Destinations:
- **Charles River Esplanade:** Enjoy a scenic ride along the river with beautiful views of the Boston skyline.
- **Emerald Necklace:** Explore this network of parks and green spaces designed by Frederick Law Olmsted.
- **Boston Harborwalk:** Ride along the waterfront and take in the sights of Boston Harbor.
- **Freedom Trail:** Follow this historic route through downtown Boston and see key landmarks on two wheels.

Whether you're a resident or a visitor, Bluebikes offers a great way to explore Boston, stay active, and contribute to a greener city.

What to See and Do

Iconic Landmarks

Boston Common

Boston Common is the oldest public park in the United States, established in 1634. Spanning 50 acres in the heart of downtown Boston, it serves as both a historical landmark and a vibrant recreational space. Initially used as a grazing ground for cattle by the town's settlers, Boston Common has a rich history that reflects the evolving nature of the city itself.

Over the centuries, the Common has played a pivotal role in many significant events. During the American Revolutionary period, it was used as a camp by British troops. The site has also hosted numerous protests, public speeches, and gatherings that have shaped the course of American history. Notably, Martin Luther King Jr. and Pope John Paul II have both delivered speeches there, underscoring its importance as a platform for public discourse.

Today, Boston Common offers a variety of attractions and activities for visitors. The Frog Pond is a popular feature, offering a splash pool for children in the summer and an ice-skating rink in the winter. The park is also home to the Soldiers and Sailors Monument, the Boston Massacre Memorial, and the Central Burying Ground, which add to its historical significance.

As the starting point of the Freedom Trail, a 2.5-mile-long path that takes visitors through 16 significant historical sites, Boston Common serves as a gateway to exploring Boston's rich heritage. With its expansive lawns, shaded walking paths, and picturesque scenery, the Common is a haven for both locals and tourists seeking relaxation and recreation. Whether you're taking a leisurely stroll, enjoying a picnic, or attending one of the many events held there, Boston Common remains a beloved and integral part of the city's landscape.

Faneuil Hall

Faneuil Hall, often referred to as the "Cradle of Liberty," is one of Boston's most famous landmarks. Built in 1742 by wealthy merchant Peter Faneuil, the hall has served as both a marketplace and a meeting hall throughout its history. It played a crucial role during the American Revolution, providing a platform for influential figures such as Samuel Adams and James Otis to speak out against British policies, inspiring the fight for independence.

Located near the waterfront, Faneuil Hall is a key component of the larger Faneuil Hall Marketplace, which includes North Market, South Market, and Quincy Market. The building itself features a distinctive red brick facade and a weather vane in the shape of a grasshopper, which has become an iconic symbol of Boston.

Today, the first floor of Faneuil Hall continues to operate as a bustling market with a variety of shops and eateries, while the second floor serves as a meeting hall that hosts various civic events and historical reenactments. The third floor is home to the Ancient and Honorable Artillery Company of Massachusetts, the oldest chartered military organization in the Western Hemisphere, which maintains a museum open to the public.

Faneuil Hall is also a stop on the Freedom Trail, making it a must-visit destination for history enthusiasts. The surrounding Faneuil Hall Marketplace offers a vibrant atmosphere with street performers, food stalls, and a wide range of retail shops, attracting millions of visitors annually. Whether you're interested in exploring its historical significance or simply enjoying the lively marketplace, Faneuil Hall provides a unique and enriching experience that encapsulates the spirit of Boston.

Quincy Market

Quincy Market, part of the historic Faneuil Hall Marketplace, is an iconic destination in downtown Boston. Opened in 1826 to accommodate the city's growing population and its need for more market space, Quincy Market is named after Josiah Quincy, the mayor of Boston at the time of its construction. The market is renowned for its Greek Revival architecture, characterized by its grand hall and long colonnades.

Initially, Quincy Market was built to relieve the overcrowded Faneuil Hall, providing additional space for vendors to sell their goods. Today, it stands as a vibrant food hall and shopping destination that attracts both locals and tourists. The central building houses a variety of food vendors offering an eclectic mix of culinary delights. From traditional New England clam chowder and lobster rolls to international cuisines and gourmet treats, the market's offerings cater to diverse tastes.

Popular vendors include Boston Chowda Co., known for its creamy clam chowder and lobster bisque, and North End Bakery, famous for its pastries and cannoli. Visitors can also enjoy sit-down meals at several restaurants, such as Salty Dog Seafood Grille & Bar, which focuses on fresh seafood, and Cheers, which offers a classic American dining experience.

Quincy Market is more than just a food hall; it's a cultural hub that hosts various events and performances, enhancing its lively atmosphere. Street performers, musicians, and entertainers frequently perform in the surrounding area, adding to the market's vibrant charm. The market also includes numerous retail shops selling souvenirs, specialty foods, and unique gifts, making it a one-stop destination for both culinary delights and shopping.

Whether you're grabbing a quick bite, shopping for unique items, or simply soaking in the historic ambiance, Quincy Market provides a quintessential Boston experience. Its blend of history, food, and entertainment makes it an essential stop for anyone visiting the city.

Paul Revere House

The Paul Revere House, located in Boston's historic North End, is one of the oldest buildings in downtown Boston, dating back to around 1680. This iconic wooden structure was the residence of Paul Revere, the American patriot renowned for his midnight ride to warn the colonial militia of the approaching British forces before the battles of Lexington and Concord.

The house is a testament to colonial architecture and has been meticulously preserved to offer visitors a glimpse into 18th-century life. Paul Revere purchased the house in 1770, and it remained his home during the critical years leading up to and following the American Revolution. The Paul Revere House is now a museum, operated by the Paul Revere Memorial Association since it opened to the public in 1908.

Visitors to the Paul Revere House can explore the modest rooms where Revere and his family lived. The museum features original furnishings, historic artifacts, and informative displays that detail Revere's life and significant contributions to American history. Highlights include a collection of Revere's silver work, personal items, and documents related to his midnight ride and other patriotic activities.

In addition to the main house, the complex includes a visitor center that provides additional context and educational resources about Revere's life and times. Knowledgeable staff and engaging exhibits offer insights into the daily lives of the Revere family and the broader historical context of the American Revolution.

The Paul Revere House is a key stop on Boston's Freedom Trail, a 2.5-mile-long path that guides visitors through 16 significant historical sites. This location not only celebrates the legacy of a national hero but also preserves an important piece of Boston's architectural and cultural heritage. Whether you're a history enthusiast or a casual visitor, the Paul Revere House offers a fascinating and educational experience.

Old North Church

The Old North Church, officially known as Christ Church in the City of Boston, is the oldest standing church building in Boston, constructed in 1723. Located in the North End, it is one of the most historically significant sites in the United States, famously associated with Paul Revere's midnight ride.

The church's steeple is where the iconic signal lanterns were hung on the night of April 18, 1775, to alert colonial militia of the British troops' approach. The phrase "One if by land, and two if by sea," referring to the signal lanterns, has become ingrained in American folklore. This event marked a pivotal moment in the lead-up to the Revolutionary War, underscoring the church's vital role in American history.

Visitors to the Old North Church can tour the historic site and learn about its rich history and architectural significance. The church features beautiful Georgian architecture, including its iconic steeple, box pews, and brass chandeliers. The interior of the church has been carefully preserved, allowing visitors to experience the atmosphere of an 18th-century colonial church.

The Old North Church also houses a museum with exhibits that delve into the church's history and its role in the American Revolution. Artifacts on display include the original church bells, which were cast in England and are still rung today, and items related to the church's congregation over the centuries.

In addition to its historical exhibits, the Old North Church offers educational programs and reenactments that bring the past to life. Knowledgeable guides provide insights into the lives of the colonial Bostonians who worshipped there and the critical events that took place within its walls.

As a key stop on the Freedom Trail, the Old North Church is an essential destination for anyone interested in American history. Its combination of historical significance, architectural beauty, and engaging exhibits makes it a compelling visit for both locals and tourists.

Massachusetts State House

The Massachusetts State House, located on Beacon Hill in Boston, is the state capitol and the seat of the Massachusetts General Court (the state legislature). Completed in 1798, it is one of the oldest and most distinguished public buildings in the United States. The State House is notable for its distinctive golden dome, which gleams prominently in the Boston skyline.

Designed by the renowned architect Charles Bulfinch, the Massachusetts State House is a masterpiece of Federal architecture. Its elegant design features a red brick facade, white columns, and a grandiose portico. The building's dome, initially made of wood and later overlaid with copper by Paul Revere's company, was gilded in 1874, giving it its iconic appearance.

The interior of the State House is equally impressive, with richly decorated chambers, historic artifacts, and beautifully preserved spaces. Visitors can tour the building to see important rooms such as the Hall of Flags, which honors Massachusetts soldiers, the House and Senate chambers, and the Governor's office. The tour provides insights into the workings of the state government and the legislative process.

The Massachusetts State House is not only a functioning government building but also a repository of the state's history. It houses numerous paintings, sculptures, and historical artifacts that reflect Massachusetts' rich cultural heritage. Notable artworks include portraits of significant figures in Massachusetts history, such as John Hancock and Samuel Adams, and murals depicting key events in the state's past.

In addition to its historical and architectural significance, the State House is an active civic center where legislative debates, public events, and state ceremonies take place. The building and its grounds are accessible to the public, offering guided tours that educate visitors about the state's political history and the functioning of its government.

As a landmark on the Freedom Trail, the Massachusetts State House is a must-visit destination for anyone interested in American history, architecture, and government. Its grand architecture, historical significance, and role as a center of state politics make it a cornerstone of Boston's heritage.

Boston Public Garden

The Boston Public Garden, established in 1837, is the first public botanical garden in the United States. Located adjacent to Boston Common, it forms part of the city's Emerald Necklace, a series of connected parks designed by landscape architect Frederick Law Olmsted. Covering 24 acres, the Public Garden is a stunning example of Victorian-era landscaping, offering a serene and picturesque escape in the heart of Boston.

The garden is renowned for its beautiful flowerbeds, which are meticulously maintained and feature a rotating display of seasonal plants and flowers. Visitors can stroll along winding pathways that meander through lush lawns, past elegant fountains, and around the garden's central lagoon. The lagoon is home to the famous Swan Boats, which have been a beloved attraction since 1877. These pedal-powered boats offer a leisurely and scenic ride, providing unique views of the garden.

Statues and monuments are scattered throughout the Boston Public Garden, adding to its historical and cultural significance. One of the most famous is the equestrian statue of George Washington, which stands proudly at the Arlington Street entrance. Other notable sculptures include the Make Way for Ducklings statues, inspired by the beloved children's book by Robert McCloskey, and the Ether Monument, commemorating the first public demonstration of ether as an anesthetic.

The Boston Public Garden is also a sanctuary for various wildlife, including ducks, swans, and other bird species. The diverse plantings and tranquil environment attract both locals and tourists seeking relaxation and natural beauty. The garden's well-maintained landscapes and vibrant flower displays make it a popular spot for picnics, leisurely walks, and photography.

Whether you're taking a ride on the Swan Boats, enjoying the colorful floral displays, or simply relaxing on a bench by the lagoon, the Boston Public Garden offers a peaceful retreat and a quintessential Boston experience. Its blend of natural beauty, historical monuments, and cultural charm make it a must-visit destination in the city.

Bunker Hill Monument

The Bunker Hill Monument, located in Charlestown, Boston, commemorates the Battle of Bunker Hill, one of the first major battles of the American Revolutionary War. The battle took place on June 17, 1775, and although the British ultimately won, the fierce resistance demonstrated by the colonial forces proved to be a significant morale booster for the revolutionaries.

The monument itself is a 221-foot granite obelisk that stands on Breed's Hill, the primary site of the battle. Construction of the monument began in 1825 and was completed in 1843. It was designed by architect Solomon Willard and built from granite quarried in nearby Quincy, Massachusetts. The Bunker Hill Monument is one of the most recognizable landmarks in Boston and offers a striking symbol of the city's revolutionary heritage.

Visitors to the Bunker Hill Monument can climb the 294 steps to the top of the obelisk, where they are rewarded with panoramic views of Boston and its surroundings. The climb is a popular activity for those who want to experience a piece of history while enjoying a unique vantage point of the city.

The Bunker Hill Monument is part of the Boston National Historical Park, which also includes a museum located at the base of the hill. The museum features exhibits on the Battle of Bunker Hill and the broader context of the American Revolution. Artifacts, maps, and interactive displays provide visitors with a comprehensive understanding of the battle and its significance.

The monument and its surrounding park area are open to the public year-round and serve as a focal point for various commemorative events, including annual ceremonies on the anniversary of the battle. The Bunker Hill Monument stands as a testament to the bravery and resilience of the early American forces and is an essential stop for anyone interested in the history of the United States.

USS Constitution

The USS Constitution, also known as "Old Ironsides," is the world's oldest commissioned naval vessel still afloat. Launched in 1797, the ship played a crucial role in the early years of the United States Navy and remains an iconic symbol of American maritime history. The USS Constitution is berthed at the Charlestown Navy Yard in Boston, part of the Boston National Historical Park.

Constructed from a design by naval architect Joshua Humphreys, the USS Constitution was one of six original frigates authorized by the Naval Act of 1794. The ship earned its nickname "Old Ironsides" during the War of 1812, when British cannonballs were seen bouncing off its sturdy hull made of a resilient combination of live oak and white oak.

Visitors to the USS Constitution can explore the ship and learn about its storied past through guided tours conducted by active-duty Navy sailors. The tours provide insights into the ship's construction, its various naval engagements, and the daily life of sailors in the early 19th century. Highlights include the ship's impressive armament, living quarters, and the captain's cabin.

The adjacent USS Constitution Museum offers a deeper dive into the ship's history and significance. The museum features interactive exhibits, artifacts, and educational programs that bring to life the experiences of those who served on the ship. Visitors can engage with hands-on displays that illustrate naval technology, shipbuilding techniques, and the strategic importance of the USS Constitution during its active years.

The USS Constitution continues to sail periodically for special events and ceremonies, maintaining its status as a commissioned ship in the U.S. Navy. This enduring legacy allows visitors to witness a living piece of history and connect with the maritime heritage of the United States.

As part of the Freedom Trail, the USS Constitution is a must-visit destination for history enthusiasts and anyone interested in naval history. Its combination of historical significance, educational value, and impressive preservation makes it a cornerstone of Boston's rich cultural landscape.

Fenway Park

Fenway Park, located in Boston's Fenway-Kenmore neighborhood, is one of the most famous and historic baseball stadiums in the United States. Home to the Boston Red Sox, Fenway Park has been a beloved landmark since it opened in 1912. Known as "America's Most Beloved Ballpark," Fenway is the oldest Major League Baseball stadium still in use, and its rich history and unique charm make it a must-visit destination for sports fans and history enthusiasts alike.

Fenway Park is renowned for its iconic features, such as the Green Monster, the towering left-field wall that stands 37 feet tall. The park's quirky dimensions and intimate seating create a unique atmosphere that is unlike any other stadium. The manual scoreboard, the lone red seat marking Ted Williams' longest home run, and the Pesky Pole all contribute to the park's storied character.

Visitors to Fenway Park can experience the magic of Red Sox games, where passionate fans create an electric atmosphere. The ballpark also offers guided tours that provide an in-depth look at its history, architecture, and memorable moments. The tours take visitors behind the scenes, offering access to areas such as the press box, the dugout, and the Green Monster seats.

In addition to baseball games, Fenway Park hosts a variety of events throughout the year, including concerts, football games, and hockey matches. The park's versatility and historic significance make it a popular venue for a wide range of activities.

The surrounding neighborhood of Fenway-Kenmore is vibrant and bustling, offering plenty of dining, shopping, and entertainment options. Yawkey Way, the street adjacent to the ballpark, transforms into a lively pedestrian area on game days, filled with vendors, street performers, and enthusiastic fans.

Fenway Park is more than just a sports venue; it is a cultural icon that embodies the spirit and history of Boston. Whether you're catching a game, taking a tour, or simply soaking in the atmosphere, a visit to Fenway Park is an unforgettable experience.

New England Aquarium

The New England Aquarium, located on Boston's Central Wharf, is one of the city's premier attractions, drawing millions of visitors each year. Since its opening in 1969, the aquarium has been dedicated to marine education, conservation, and research, offering an engaging and educational experience for visitors of all ages.

One of the main highlights of the New England Aquarium is the Giant Ocean Tank, a four-story cylindrical tank that serves as the centerpiece of the facility. The tank houses a vibrant coral reef ecosystem, featuring a diverse array of marine life, including sea turtles, sharks, stingrays, and hundreds of tropical fish species. Visitors can observe the tank from multiple levels, gaining different perspectives of the underwater world.

The aquarium is also home to the popular penguin exhibit, where visitors can watch playful penguins frolic and swim in a carefully recreated natural habitat. The exhibit features several species of penguins, including African penguins and rockhopper penguins, and provides insights into their behaviors and conservation status.

Other notable exhibits include the Amazon Rainforest, showcasing freshwater species such as piranhas and anacondas, and the Edge of the Sea tidepool touch tank, where visitors can interact with marine invertebrates like starfish, sea urchins, and crabs. The New Balance Foundation Marine Mammal Center is another favorite, offering daily presentations and feedings of California sea lions and northern fur seals.

The New England Aquarium is committed to conservation and sustainability, actively participating in marine research and rescue efforts. The facility's educational programs and interactive exhibits aim to inspire visitors to appreciate and protect the ocean and its inhabitants.

In addition to its exhibits, the aquarium offers whale watching tours from spring through fall. These excursions provide an opportunity to see humpback whales, finback whales, and other marine wildlife in their natural habitats, guided by knowledgeable naturalists.

With its captivating exhibits, commitment to conservation, and educational programs, the New England Aquarium offers a fascinating and enriching experience. Whether you're a marine enthusiast or simply looking for a fun and informative outing, the aquarium is a must-visit destination in Boston.

Boston Tea Party Ships & Museum

The Boston Tea Party Ships & Museum, located on the Congress Street Bridge in Boston, offers a dynamic and immersive experience that brings one of the most pivotal events in American history to life. The museum is dedicated to the Boston Tea Party of December 16, 1773, a significant act of defiance against British rule that helped spark the American Revolution.

Visitors to the museum can engage in interactive exhibits and live reenactments that provide a vivid portrayal of the events leading up to the Tea Party. The experience begins with a dramatic meeting at the replica of the Old South Meeting House, where costumed actors representing Samuel Adams and other patriots discuss the oppressive Tea Act and rally the audience to take action.

One of the main highlights of the museum is the opportunity to board authentically restored ships, the Eleanor and the Beaver, which are docked at the museum's wharf. These ships are meticulously crafted replicas of the original vessels that transported the controversial tea. Onboard, visitors can participate in the symbolic act of throwing crates of tea overboard, just as the colonists did in 1773, providing a hands-on understanding of this historic protest.

The museum also features an array of artifacts, including one of the original tea chests recovered from the harbor, historical documents, and interactive displays that delve into the broader context of the American Revolution. The multi-sensory exhibits, such as holographic presentations and immersive audiovisual experiences, effectively transport visitors back to the 18th century.

In addition to the historical exhibits, the Boston Tea Party Ships & Museum offers a charming tea room, Abigail's Tea Room, where visitors can enjoy colonial-era refreshments and learn about the importance of tea in 18th-century America. The museum shop provides a variety of themed souvenirs, books, and educational materials.

The Boston Tea Party Ships & Museum is not only an educational attraction but also a compelling storytelling experience that makes history accessible and engaging for visitors of all ages. Its blend of interactive elements, authentic replicas, and historical artifacts offers a unique way to explore and understand the roots of American independence.

John Hancock Tower

The John Hancock Tower, officially known as 200 Clarendon, is a striking landmark in Boston's Back Bay neighborhood. Completed in 1976, it stands as the tallest building in New England, reaching a height of 790 feet with 62 floors. Designed by the renowned architectural firm Pei Cobb Freed & Partners, the tower is an exemplary piece of modernist architecture, characterized by its sleek glass facade and minimalist design.

The building's reflective glass exterior is one of its most distinctive features. The curtain wall mirrors the surrounding cityscape, creating an ever-changing mosaic of Boston's skyline, the Charles River, and the historic Trinity Church, which sits adjacent to the tower. This interplay between the old and the new symbolizes Boston's blend of historic charm and contemporary innovation.

The John Hancock Tower is primarily an office building, housing a variety of businesses and professional services. However, its architectural significance and commanding presence make it a notable point of interest for both locals and tourists. The tower's design emphasizes simplicity and elegance, and it has received numerous accolades for its aesthetic and structural qualities.

Originally, the building faced significant engineering challenges, particularly with the stability of its glass panels, which led to several redesigns and repairs. These issues were eventually resolved, and the tower now stands as a testament to modern engineering and design resilience.

Although the John Hancock Tower does not have an observation deck open to the public, its location in Copley Square provides ample opportunities to appreciate its grandeur. The nearby Boston Public Library, Copley Square, and Trinity Church offer picturesque views of the tower, making it a frequent subject for photographers and architecture enthusiasts.

The tower's impact on the Boston skyline is profound, serving as a central marker in the city's architectural landscape. Its presence underscores Boston's role as a hub of business, culture, and innovation. The John Hancock Tower remains a symbol of the city's progress and its enduring capacity to blend historical significance with modern development.

Boston Public Library

The Boston Public Library (BPL), located in the heart of Copley Square, is not only a beacon of knowledge but also a stunning architectural gem. Founded in 1848, the BPL was the first large free municipal library in the United States, marking a significant milestone in the accessibility of knowledge to the public. The library's main building, known as the McKim Building, was completed in 1895 and is a masterpiece of Renaissance Revival architecture.

Visitors are immediately struck by the grandeur of the entrance, which is adorned with inscriptions by renowned authors and philosophers, reflecting the library's dedication to learning and culture. Upon entering, the vastness and beauty of the interior spaces captivate the imagination. The Bates Hall reading room, with its high, coffered ceiling and rows of green lamps, is one of the most iconic spaces in the library, offering a serene environment for study and reflection.

Art lovers will appreciate the murals by John Singer Sargent, which depict the triumph of religion and other allegorical themes, adding a layer of artistic depth to the library's already rich environment. The BPL also houses an extensive collection of rare books, manuscripts, and special collections, making it a destination for scholars and history enthusiasts alike.

Beyond its role as a library, the BPL serves as a cultural hub for the community, hosting numerous events, exhibitions, and public programs throughout the year. The tranquil courtyard, inspired by an Italian monastery, provides a peaceful retreat from the city's bustle, where visitors can relax and enjoy the beauty of the surroundings.

The Boston Public Library is more than just a place to borrow books; it's a cultural institution that embodies the spirit of education, art, and community in the heart of Boston.

Arnold Arboretum

The Arnold Arboretum, a 281-acre botanical garden managed by Harvard University, is a cherished green space located in the Jamaica Plain and Roslindale neighborhoods of Boston. Founded in 1872, the Arboretum is one of the oldest public arboretums in North America and serves as a living museum, showcasing an extensive collection of trees, shrubs, and plants from around the world.

Visitors to the Arnold Arboretum are greeted by a diverse landscape that changes with the seasons. Spring brings vibrant blossoms from cherry trees, magnolias, and lilacs, while the summer months showcase lush greenery and colorful flower beds. In autumn, the Arboretum is transformed into a tapestry of reds, oranges, and yellows as the leaves change, making it a popular destination for fall foliage enthusiasts. Even in winter, the Arboretum offers a peaceful retreat, with snow-covered trees creating a serene environment for a quiet walk.

The Arboretum is designed as a place for both education and recreation. Miles of walking paths wind through the gardens, allowing visitors to explore different plant collections and enjoy the natural beauty at their own pace. The Arboretum also offers educational programs, guided tours, and special events, such as the annual Lilac Sunday, which celebrates the blooming of the extensive lilac collection.

One of the highlights of the Arboretum is the Bonsai and Penjing Collection, which features miniature trees that are meticulously cared for and displayed to showcase the ancient art of bonsai. The Arboretum's mission to promote the understanding and appreciation of plants is evident in the careful curation of its collections and the educational opportunities it provides.

Whether you're a botany enthusiast, a nature lover, or simply looking for a peaceful escape from the city, the Arnold Arboretum offers a unique and enriching experience that connects visitors with the natural world in a profound way.

The Boston Harbor Islands National and State Park

The Boston Harbor Islands National and State Park is a unique destination offering a blend of natural beauty, historical significance, and recreational opportunities. Located just a short ferry ride from downtown Boston, the park consists of 34 islands and peninsulas scattered throughout Boston Harbor, each with its own distinct character and attractions.

One of the most popular islands to visit is Georges Island, known for Fort Warren, a well-preserved Civil War-era fort that played a crucial role in the defense of Boston Harbor. Visitors can explore the fort's tunnels, barracks, and parade grounds while learning about its history through guided tours and informational displays. The island's open spaces also provide scenic spots for picnicking, with panoramic views of the harbor and the Boston skyline.

Another favorite is Spectacle Island, which offers a more relaxed experience. Once a landfill, Spectacle Island has been transformed into a green oasis with five miles of hiking trails, sandy beaches, and a visitor center. The island's highest point provides a stunning 360-degree view of the harbor, making it an ideal spot for photography or simply taking in the natural surroundings.

For those interested in outdoor activities, the Boston Harbor Islands offer opportunities for hiking, bird watching, kayaking, and even camping. Peddocks Island, one of the larger islands, features both campsites and historic structures, including remnants of Fort Andrews, used during World War II.

The islands are not just about outdoor adventure; they also offer a glimpse into New England's maritime history and the area's natural ecosystem. Rangers and volunteers often provide educational programs, guided walks, and interpretive exhibits that enhance the visitor experience.

Accessible from spring through early fall, the Boston Harbor Islands National and State Park is a must-visit destination for those looking to escape the hustle and bustle of the city while still staying close to Boston's historic and cultural offerings.

Museums and Cultural Institutions

Museum of Fine Arts, Boston

The Museum of Fine Arts, Boston (MFA) is one of the most comprehensive art museums in the world, with a collection that spans nearly 500,000 works of art. Founded in 1870 and relocated to its current location on Huntington Avenue in 1909, the MFA is a cultural cornerstone in Boston, offering a rich and diverse array of exhibitions and programs.

The MFA's collection is vast and varied, encompassing pieces from ancient Egyptian artifacts to contemporary art. Highlights include its impressive holdings of Impressionist paintings, featuring works by Monet, Renoir, and Van Gogh. The museum is also renowned for its extensive collection of American art, including significant pieces by John Singleton Copley, Winslow Homer, and John Singer Sargent.

One of the museum's most celebrated collections is its Japanese art, one of the largest and finest outside Japan. The MFA's Asian art collection includes over 100,000 objects, ranging from ancient Chinese bronzes to contemporary Japanese prints. Additionally, the museum boasts significant holdings in European, African, and Oceanic art, making it a truly global institution.

The MFA is not only a repository of visual art but also a vibrant center for cultural education. It offers a wide range of programs for all ages, including art classes, lectures, film screenings, and special events. The museum's commitment to education is evident in its interactive exhibits and its acclaimed Art of the Americas Wing, which offers an immersive experience into the history and culture of the Americas.

The museum's architecture is also noteworthy. The original neoclassical building has been expanded over the years, including the recent addition of the modern Art of the Americas Wing and the Linde Family Wing for Contemporary Art. These expansions have enhanced the museum's ability to showcase its extensive collections and provide dynamic spaces for visitors.

Whether you're an art enthusiast or a casual visitor, the Museum of Fine Arts, Boston offers a captivating journey through the history of art. Its diverse collections, educational programs, and stunning architecture make it a must-visit destination in Boston.

Isabella Stewart Gardner Museum

The Isabella Stewart Gardner Museum, located in Boston's Fenway-Kenmore neighborhood, is a unique and enchanting cultural institution. Founded by the eccentric and visionary art collector Isabella Stewart Gardner, the museum opened its doors in 1903. Housed in a Venetian-style palazzo, the museum reflects Gardner's eclectic taste and passion for art, travel, and culture.

The museum's collection includes more than 2,500 works of art, spanning European, Asian, and American art. Gardner's personal touch is evident throughout the museum, with each room meticulously curated to reflect her aesthetic vision. The collection features masterpieces by renowned artists such as Titian, Rembrandt, Vermeer, and Sargent, alongside ancient artifacts, rare books, and decorative arts.

One of the museum's most striking features is its central courtyard, a lush, plant-filled oasis inspired by Italian Renaissance gardens. The courtyard, visible from nearly every room in the museum, creates a serene and contemplative atmosphere, inviting visitors to pause and reflect.

The Isabella Stewart Gardner Museum is also famous for a dramatic art heist that occurred in 1990. Thirteen pieces, including works by Vermeer and Rembrandt, were stolen and have never been recovered. Empty frames still hang in their original locations, serving as a poignant reminder of the missing art and the ongoing search for its return.

In addition to its permanent collection, the museum hosts rotating exhibitions, concerts, lectures, and educational programs. The Renzo Piano-designed addition, completed in 2012, includes a contemporary gallery space, a music performance hall, and a greenhouse, enhancing the museum's ability to offer diverse cultural experiences.

Gardner's will stipulated that the arrangement of the collection should remain unchanged, preserving her vision for future generations. This directive ensures that visitors experience the museum much as she intended, providing an intimate glimpse into her world.

The Isabella Stewart Gardner Museum offers a captivating blend of art, history, and horticulture, making it a must-visit destination in Boston. Its unique setting, extraordinary collection, and the intriguing story behind its creation make it a cultural treasure.

Boston Children's Museum

The Boston Children's Museum, located on Fort Point Channel in Boston's Seaport District, is one of the oldest and largest children's museums in the world. Established in 1913, the museum has a long history of engaging young minds through interactive exhibits and educational programs that encourage exploration, creativity, and learning.

The museum is designed with a focus on hands-on learning, offering a variety of exhibits that cater to children of all ages. One of the most iconic features is the New Balance Climb, a three-story climbing structure that challenges children to navigate through a series of interconnected platforms and ropes, promoting physical activity and problem-solving skills.

Another popular exhibit is the Japanese House, a fully equipped two-story townhouse transported from Kyoto, Japan. This exhibit offers children and families a glimpse into Japanese culture and daily life, fostering cultural understanding and appreciation.

The Construction Zone allows children to don hard hats and work with real tools in a safe, supervised environment, helping them learn about building and engineering concepts. The museum also features a science playground, where kids can experiment with water, air, and physical forces through interactive displays.

Art Studio and KidStage provide creative outlets for artistic expression and dramatic play. In the Art Studio, children can engage in various art projects, while KidStage offers live performances and opportunities for kids to participate in theatrical productions.

The Boston Children's Museum is dedicated to promoting diversity and inclusion through its exhibits and programs. The Puzzles & Mysteries exhibit, for example, encourages children to think critically and solve problems, while the PlaySpace is designed specifically for toddlers, ensuring that even the youngest visitors have a stimulating environment to explore.

In addition to its permanent exhibits, the museum hosts a variety of temporary exhibits and special events throughout the year. Educational programs, including school visits, summer camps, and family workshops, further enhance the museum's mission to inspire a lifelong love of learning.

The Boston Children's Museum is a vibrant and dynamic space where children can learn, play, and grow. Its commitment to hands-on, experiential learning makes it a beloved institution for families in Boston and beyond, providing a fun and enriching experience for all who visit.

Museum of Science

The Museum of Science in Boston, located along the Charles River, is one of the most prestigious science museums in the world. Established in 1830, it has evolved into a leading institution dedicated to inspiring a lifelong love of science in visitors of all ages. The museum's mission is to promote a greater understanding of the natural and human-made world through exhibits, programs, and educational outreach.

One of the museum's most iconic features is the Charles Hayden Planetarium, which offers state-of-the-art presentations on astronomy and space exploration. The planetarium's immersive shows use cutting-edge technology to provide stunning visuals and informative narratives about the cosmos.

Another highlight is the Butterfly Garden, an indoor conservatory where visitors can walk among free-flying butterflies and observe their behavior up close. This exhibit not only delights visitors but also educates them about the life cycles and ecological importance of butterflies.

The museum boasts a wide range of interactive exhibits that cover various scientific disciplines. The Hall of Human Life explores human biology and health, offering hands-on activities that allow visitors to learn about their bodies and how they function. The Engineering Design Workshop encourages creativity and problem-solving by letting visitors build and test their own designs.

The Museum of Science is also home to the Mugar Omni Theater, which features a five-story domed screen that presents large-format films on topics ranging from natural history to space exploration. These films offer breathtaking visuals and engaging storytelling that enhance the learning experience.

The museum's commitment to education extends beyond its exhibits. It offers numerous educational programs, including school field trips, summer camps, and after-school programs. The Traveling Programs bring science education to schools and communities throughout New England.

The Museum of Science regularly hosts special exhibitions, bringing in unique and informative displays from around the world. These temporary exhibits ensure that there is always something new to discover, making each visit to the museum a fresh and exciting experience.

With its comprehensive exhibits, innovative programs, and dedication to public education, the Museum of Science is a cornerstone of Boston's cultural and educational landscape. It provides a stimulating environment where visitors can explore, learn, and be inspired by the wonders of science.

Harvard Museum of Natural History

The Harvard Museum of Natural History, located in Cambridge, Massachusetts, is a must-visit destination for anyone interested in the natural world. Established in 1998, the museum combines the collections of three renowned research museums at Harvard University: the Harvard University Herbaria, the Museum of Comparative Zoology, and the Mineralogical and Geological Museum. Together, these collections offer an unparalleled glimpse into the diversity of life on Earth, both past and present.

One of the museum's most famous exhibits is the Glass Flowers collection. Officially known as the Ware Collection of Blaschka Glass Models of Plants, this exhibit features over 4,000 incredibly detailed glass models of plants and flowers created by Leopold and Rudolf Blaschka. These models were crafted between 1887 and 1936 and are renowned for their scientific accuracy and artistic beauty.

Another highlight is the Great Mammal Hall, which showcases an impressive array of mammal specimens from around the world. The hall is designed to demonstrate the vast diversity and evolutionary history of mammals, featuring everything from tiny rodents to the towering skeleton of a whale.

The museum also houses a significant collection of minerals, gems, and meteorites. The Earth and Planetary Sciences Gallery displays stunning specimens, including sparkling gemstones, intricate mineral formations, and meteorites that offer insights into the formation of the solar system.

The Harvard Museum of Natural History is dedicated to public education and offers a variety of programs for visitors of all ages. These include lectures, workshops, and interactive activities designed to engage and inspire a deeper understanding of natural history. The museum also provides resources and training for educators to help bring natural history into the classroom.

The museum's exhibitions are designed to be accessible and engaging, providing hands-on learning opportunities and interactive displays that captivate visitors. The combination of historical artifacts, scientific research, and modern educational techniques makes the Harvard Museum of Natural History a dynamic and enriching experience.

Whether you're fascinated by botanical art, intrigued by the animal kingdom, or captivated by the mysteries of geology, the Harvard Museum of Natural History offers something for everyone. Its comprehensive collections and educational programs make it a vital cultural resource and an essential stop for anyone visiting the Boston area.

MIT Museum

The MIT Museum, located in Cambridge, Massachusetts, serves as a window into the world of innovation and technology that defines the Massachusetts Institute of Technology (MIT). Founded in 1971, the museum aims to engage the public with MIT's groundbreaking research and discoveries, inspiring visitors to appreciate and explore the intersections of science, technology, engineering, and art.

One of the key attractions of the MIT Museum is its extensive collection of holography. As a pioneer in the field, MIT has amassed one of the largest collections of holograms in the world. The museum's Holography Collection showcases both scientific applications and artistic uses of holography, demonstrating the breadth and versatility of this fascinating technology.

Robotics is another major focus at the MIT Museum. The museum features exhibits on the history and development of robotics, highlighting MIT's contributions to the field. Visitors can see a variety of robots, from early prototypes to advanced autonomous machines, and learn about the cutting-edge research that is pushing the boundaries of what robots can do.

The museum also explores the field of artificial intelligence (AI), offering insights into how AI is developed and applied. Interactive exhibits and demonstrations allow visitors to engage with AI technology and understand its impact on everyday life and future possibilities.

The Gestural Engineering exhibit, featuring the work of kinetic artist Arthur Ganson, is a unique blend of art and engineering. Ganson's whimsical and intricate mechanical sculptures are mesmerizing to watch and provide a creative perspective on the principles of mechanics and movement.

In addition to its permanent exhibits, the MIT Museum hosts temporary exhibitions that cover a wide range of topics related to science, technology, and innovation. These exhibitions often feature the latest research from MIT's labs, providing visitors with a glimpse into the future of technology.

The MIT Museum is committed to education and public engagement, offering a variety of programs, workshops, and events. These include the popular Cambridge Science Festival, a multi-day celebration of science and technology that features interactive exhibits, demonstrations, and talks.

Through its exhibits and programs, the MIT Museum fosters a deeper understanding of the role of technology and innovation in shaping our world. It provides an inspiring and educational experience for visitors of all ages, highlighting the exciting work being done at MIT and its impact on society.

John F. Kennedy Presidential Library and Museum

The John F. Kennedy Presidential Library and Museum, located on Columbia Point in the Dorchester neighborhood of Boston, is dedicated to the life, legacy, and leadership of the 35th President of the United States, John F. Kennedy. Designed by the renowned architect I.M. Pei, the library and museum opened to the public in 1979 and stands as a striking tribute to one of America's most beloved presidents.

The museum's exhibits are thoughtfully curated to provide a comprehensive look at JFK's life and career, from his early years and military service to his presidency and enduring impact on American history. Visitors can explore multimedia exhibits that include rare photographs, personal artifacts, and historical documents. Notable displays include Kennedy's handwritten notes, his Oval Office desk, and the famous rocking chair he used during his presidency.

One of the museum's key attractions is the recreated 1960 Democratic National Convention, where visitors can experience the excitement of JFK's nomination and acceptance speech. Another highlight is the space exploration exhibit, which celebrates Kennedy's pivotal role in launching the United States' space program, culminating in the moon landing in 1969.

The museum also features a theater that screens a documentary film about Kennedy's life and times, providing a powerful introduction to his story. Interactive exhibits allow visitors to engage with key moments of Kennedy's presidency, including the Cuban Missile Crisis and the Civil Rights Movement.

In addition to its exhibits, the John F. Kennedy Presidential Library hosts a variety of public programs, including lectures, panel discussions, and educational activities. The library's extensive archives are a valuable resource for scholars and researchers, containing millions of documents, photographs, and recordings related to JFK's life and presidency.

The museum's location on the waterfront offers stunning views of the Boston skyline and the harbor, enhancing the visitor experience. Whether you're a history buff, a student, or a curious traveler, the John F. Kennedy Presidential Library and Museum provides an inspiring and educational journey through the life of a remarkable leader.

Boston African American National Historic Site

The Boston African American National Historic Site, located in the Beacon Hill neighborhood, is a collection of historic sites that collectively tell the story of Boston's 19th-century African American community and their significant contributions to the abolitionist movement and the fight for civil rights. The site, established in 1980, is managed by the National Park Service and offers a unique window into this critical chapter of American history.

One of the central features of the site is the Black Heritage Trail, a 1.6-mile walking tour that connects 14 historical landmarks significant to Boston's

African American history. The trail includes homes, churches, and schools that were integral to the community's life and activism.

The African Meeting House, built in 1806, is the oldest surviving black church building in the United States and served as a vital hub for community gatherings, worship, and activism. It was here that prominent abolitionists, including Frederick Douglass and William Lloyd Garrison, spoke out against slavery and advocated for equal rights.

Adjacent to the African Meeting House is the Abiel Smith School, the first public school for African American children in Boston. Today, it serves as a museum and educational center, offering exhibits on the history of the school and the broader struggle for educational equality.

The homes of notable figures such as Lewis and Harriet Hayden are also part of the historic site. The Hayden House was a stop on the Underground Railroad, providing refuge to enslaved individuals seeking freedom. Visitors can learn about the courageous efforts of the Haydens and other members of the community who risked their lives to help others escape slavery.

The Boston African American National Historic Site provides guided tours that offer in-depth insights into the history and significance of each landmark. The tours, led by knowledgeable park rangers, highlight the stories of resilience, resistance, and achievement that define the African American experience in Boston.

Visiting the Boston African American National Historic Site is a powerful and educational experience, offering a deeper understanding of the city's rich history and the pivotal role its African American community played in shaping the nation's quest for freedom and equality.

Institute of Contemporary Art

The Institute of Contemporary Art (ICA), located on the Boston waterfront in the Seaport District, is a leading cultural institution dedicated to showcasing contemporary art in all its forms. Founded in 1936, the ICA has evolved into a vibrant hub for innovative art, featuring cutting-edge exhibitions, performances, and educational programs that engage and inspire visitors.

The ICA's striking building, designed by the architectural firm Diller Scofidio + Renfro, opened in 2006 and has become an architectural landmark in its own right. The building's sleek, modern design includes a cantilevered glass gallery that extends over the harbor, providing stunning views of the waterfront and the city skyline. This dynamic space reflects the ICA's commitment to contemporary art and creates a visually stimulating environment for visitors.

The museum's exhibition program features works by emerging and established artists from around the world, spanning a wide range of media, including painting, sculpture, photography, video, and performance art. The ICA is known for its thought-provoking and often challenging exhibitions that explore current issues and ideas, offering a platform for artistic experimentation and dialogue.

In addition to its rotating exhibitions, the ICA houses a permanent collection that includes works by influential contemporary artists such as Kara Walker, Cindy Sherman, and Mark Bradford. The collection reflects the museum's dedication to capturing the evolving landscape of contemporary art and providing a historical context for current artistic practices.

The ICA also hosts a variety of performances, screenings, and events that complement its visual art exhibitions. The Barbara Lee Family Foundation Theater, a flexible performance space within the museum, presents dance, music, theater, and film programs that highlight innovative and interdisciplinary approaches to art.

Education is a core component of the ICA's mission, and the museum offers a range of programs designed to engage audiences of all ages. These include artist talks, workshops, and community partnerships that foster a deeper understanding and appreciation of contemporary art. The ICA's Teen Arts Program is particularly notable, providing young people with opportunities to explore their creativity and connect with professional artists.

With its dynamic exhibitions, innovative programming, and commitment to education, the Institute of Contemporary Art is a cornerstone of Boston's cultural landscape. It offers visitors a stimulating and ever-changing experience, reflecting the diverse and evolving nature of contemporary art.

Nichols House Museum

The Nichols House Museum, located on historic Beacon Hill in Boston, offers a fascinating glimpse into the life of a prominent Boston family during the late 19th and early 20th centuries. The museum is housed in a four-story townhouse built in 1804 and designed by Charles Bulfinch, a renowned architect who played a significant role in shaping Boston's architectural heritage.

The Nichols House was the home of Rose Standish Nichols, a noted landscape architect, suffragist, and pacifist, from 1885 until her death in 1960. The house was converted into a museum in 1961 to preserve and share the history of the Nichols family and the broader social and cultural history of Boston's elite during this period.

Visitors to the Nichols House Museum can explore the meticulously preserved rooms, which are furnished with the Nichols family's original belongings, including furniture, decorative arts, and personal artifacts. The museum's collection features a mix of American and European furnishings, fine art, and Oriental rugs, reflecting the sophisticated tastes and cosmopolitan lifestyle of the Nichols family.

The museum's guided tours offer insights into the daily life and interests of Rose Standish Nichols and her family. Highlights include the formal parlor, where the Nichols entertained guests; the dining room, adorned with fine china and silverware; and the library, which houses an extensive collection of books and periodicals. The bedrooms and private quarters reveal the more intimate aspects of the family's life, showcasing personal items and family heirlooms.

In addition to its focus on the Nichols family, the museum offers a broader historical context, exploring themes such as the development of Beacon Hill, the role of women in the early 20th century, and the influence of global travel and cultural exchange on Boston society.

The Nichols House Museum also hosts a variety of educational programs and events, including lectures, workshops, and seasonal tours that highlight different aspects of the house and its history. These programs aim to engage the community and foster a deeper appreciation for Boston's rich cultural heritage.

With its well-preserved interiors, rich collections, and engaging programs, the Nichols House Museum offers a unique and intimate experience of Boston's history. It provides a valuable window into the lives of one of the city's prominent families and the cultural landscape of Beacon Hill during a transformative period in American history.

Theaters and Performances

Boston Opera House

The Boston Opera House, located in the heart of Boston's Theatre District, is a stunning architectural gem and one of the city's premier venues for performing arts. Originally opened in 1928 as the B.F. Keith Memorial Theatre, the building was designed by the renowned theater architect Thomas W. Lamb. It was initially a vaudeville house and later became a movie palace before being meticulously restored and reopened as the Boston Opera House in 2004.

The restoration of the Boston Opera House returned it to its former glory, highlighting its lavish Beaux-Arts design. The interior features opulent marble columns, ornate plasterwork, crystal chandeliers, and a grand staircase, making it a breathtaking setting for any performance. The auditorium, with its rich red and gold color scheme, offers excellent sightlines and acoustics, enhancing the audience's experience.

Today, the Boston Opera House hosts a wide range of performances, including Broadway shows, ballets, operas, and concerts. It is the home of the Boston Ballet, one of the leading ballet companies in the United States, known for its annual production of "The Nutcracker," which has become a beloved holiday tradition for many families.

The venue also regularly presents touring Broadway productions, bringing the best of New York's theater scene to Boston. Audiences can enjoy a variety of genres, from classic musicals to contemporary plays, in this elegant setting.

In addition to its regular programming, the Boston Opera House is available for private events, offering a unique and historic backdrop for weddings, corporate events, and other special occasions.

The Boston Opera House is not just a performance venue; it is a testament to the city's rich cultural history and its ongoing commitment to the arts. Whether attending a ballet, a Broadway show, or a special event, visitors to the Boston Opera House are sure to be impressed by its architectural beauty and the high quality of its performances.

Wang Theatre

The Wang Theatre, part of the Boch Center, is one of Boston's most historic and grand performing arts venues. Located on Tremont Street in the Theatre District, the Wang Theatre originally opened in 1925 as the Metropolitan Theatre. It was later renamed the Music Hall and then the Wang Theatre in 1983, in recognition of a generous donation from the Wang family.

Designed by the prominent theater architect Clarence Blackall, the Wang Theatre is an architectural masterpiece, featuring a lavishly decorated interior that combines elements of Renaissance and Baroque styles. The grand lobby, with its sweeping marble staircases, gilded ceilings, and ornate chandeliers, creates a majestic entrance that sets the tone for the performances within.

The auditorium is one of the largest in New England, seating over 3,600 people. Its design ensures excellent acoustics and clear sightlines from every seat, making it an ideal venue for a wide range of performances. The theater's proscenium stage has hosted countless Broadway shows, concerts, ballets, and other major events, drawing audiences from across the region.

The Wang Theatre is renowned for its rich history and cultural significance. It has been the venue for numerous memorable performances, including shows by world-famous artists and large-scale Broadway productions. The theater's commitment to the arts is evident in its diverse programming, which includes classical music concerts, contemporary dance, popular music acts, and family-friendly shows.

In addition to its regular performances, the Wang Theatre is home to various educational and community programs. The Boch Center's City Spotlights Leadership Program, for example, empowers young people through arts and leadership training, using the theater as a platform for personal and artistic growth.

The Wang Theatre's opulent design, impressive size, and commitment to cultural enrichment make it a cornerstone of Boston's arts scene. Whether attending a Broadway blockbuster, a classical concert, or a community event, visitors to the Wang Theatre are sure to be captivated by its beauty and the quality of its performances.

Orpheum Theatre

The Orpheum Theatre, located on Hamilton Place in downtown Boston, is one of the city's oldest and most storied entertainment venues. Originally opened in 1852 as the Boston Music Hall, it was the first home of the Boston Symphony Orchestra. The theater was extensively remodeled and reopened as the Orpheum Theatre in 1900, and it has since become a beloved institution for live music and entertainment.

The Orpheum Theatre boasts a rich history and has played a significant role in Boston's cultural life for over a century. Its neoclassical design, featuring a grand façade with Corinthian columns and an elegant interior adorned with decorative plasterwork and ornate chandeliers, reflects the architectural grandeur of its era. The theater's intimate seating arrangement, with a capacity of approximately 2,700, ensures a close connection between the performers and the audience.

Throughout its history, the Orpheum Theatre has hosted an impressive array of performances, from classical music and opera to vaudeville, theater, and popular music concerts. In the 20th century, it became a key venue for rock and roll, hosting legendary artists such as Bob Dylan, Led Zeppelin, and The Rolling Stones. Today, it continues to attract top musical acts and is a favorite venue for concerts, comedy shows, and special events.

The Orpheum Theatre is known for its excellent acoustics, making it a preferred location for live music performances. Its historic charm and vibrant atmosphere provide a unique concert-going experience that distinguishes it from modern venues.

In addition to its rich musical heritage, the Orpheum Theatre is an important part of Boston's cultural fabric, hosting a variety of events that cater to diverse audiences. The theater's location in the heart of downtown Boston makes it easily accessible and a popular destination for both locals and tourists.

The Orpheum Theatre's enduring legacy, historic ambiance, and diverse programming make it a treasured landmark in Boston. Whether attending a rock concert, a stand-up comedy show, or a special event, visitors to the Orpheum Theatre are sure to appreciate its historical significance and the memorable experiences it offers.

Cutler Majestic Theatre

The Cutler Majestic Theatre, located in Boston's vibrant Theatre District, is a historic gem that blends old-world charm with modern sophistication. Built in 1903, the theater was originally designed by the prominent architect John Galen Howard as the second home for the "second" Old Howard Athenaeum. It was conceived as a vaudeville house but soon transitioned to hosting a variety of performances, including opera, theater, and films.

The theater's architecture is a stunning example of Beaux-Arts design, featuring a grand façade with ornate detailing, intricate moldings, and a beautifully decorated interior. The auditorium boasts rich red and gold color schemes, with luxurious seating and excellent sightlines, creating an intimate yet grand atmosphere for theatergoers.

Renovated and reopened by Emerson College in 1989, the Cutler Majestic Theatre now serves as a premier venue for both college and professional productions. It hosts a wide range of performances, including plays, musicals, dance performances, and concerts. The theater is renowned for its acoustics and technical capabilities, making it an ideal setting for high-quality productions.

In addition to its role as a performance venue, the Cutler Majestic Theatre is committed to arts education and community engagement. Emerson College uses the space to support its performing arts programs, providing students with opportunities to learn and perform in a professional environment. The theater also collaborates with local arts organizations to offer a diverse array of programming that appeals to audiences of all ages and backgrounds.

The Cutler Majestic Theatre's blend of historic elegance and modern functionality makes it a beloved cultural landmark in Boston. Whether attending a student production, a touring Broadway show, or a classical concert, visitors are sure to be impressed by the theater's ambiance and the quality of its performances.

Emerson Colonial Theatre

The Emerson Colonial Theatre, located on Boylston Street in Boston's Theatre District, is a storied venue with a rich history of showcasing Broadway premieres and theatrical excellence. Opened in 1900, it is one of the oldest continuously operating theaters in the United States and has played a significant role in the development of American theater.

The theater's design, by architect Clarence Blackall, is a masterpiece of Beaux-Arts architecture. Its elegant exterior and opulent interior, featuring intricate plasterwork, grand chandeliers, and a sweeping staircase, create a luxurious setting for audiences. The auditorium, with its plush seating and excellent acoustics, provides an intimate yet grand environment for theatergoers.

The Emerson Colonial Theatre has been the site of many significant theatrical premieres, including "Porgy and Bess," "Oklahoma!," "Follies," and "A Little Night Music." Its stage has hosted legendary performers and productions, earning it a reputation as a premier venue for pre-Broadway tryouts and major theatrical events.

In 2018, the theater underwent a meticulous restoration, returning it to its former glory while updating its facilities to meet modern standards. This renovation preserved the historic charm of the venue while enhancing the audience experience with improved seating, acoustics, and technical capabilities.

Today, the Emerson Colonial Theatre continues to host a diverse array of performances, including Broadway shows, concerts, comedy acts, and special events. It remains a vital part of Boston's cultural landscape, attracting theater enthusiasts from across the region and beyond.

The theater is also a key component of Emerson College's commitment to the arts. It serves as a venue for student productions and educational programs, providing invaluable opportunities for students to engage with the performing arts in a professional setting.

With its rich history, stunning architecture, and ongoing contributions to the arts, the Emerson Colonial Theatre is a beloved cultural institution in Boston. Whether attending a world premiere or a beloved classic, visitors are sure to be captivated by the theater's ambiance and the quality of its performances.

Wilbur Theatre

The Wilbur Theatre, located on Tremont Street in Boston's Theatre District, is a historic venue renowned for its intimate setting and diverse programming. Opened in 1914, the theater was designed by architect

Clarence Blackall, who also designed several other notable theaters in Boston. The Wilbur's design was inspired by the English music hall tradition, featuring a smaller, more intimate auditorium that fosters a close connection between performers and audiences.

The theater's Beaux-Arts architecture is characterized by its elegant façade, ornate detailing, and a beautifully decorated interior. The Wilbur's seating capacity of around 1,200 provides an intimate and comfortable environment, making it an ideal venue for a wide range of performances.

Over the years, the Wilbur Theatre has hosted a variety of entertainment, including plays, musicals, concerts, and comedy shows. In recent years, it has become particularly well-known as a premier venue for stand-up comedy, attracting some of the biggest names in the industry. Comedians such as Jerry Seinfeld, Louis C.K., and John Mulaney have performed at the Wilbur, solidifying its reputation as a top destination for comedy in Boston.

In addition to comedy, the Wilbur Theatre's programming includes live music performances, theatrical productions, and special events. Its versatile stage and excellent acoustics make it a popular choice for both performers and audiences.

The Wilbur Theatre's central location in the Theatre District makes it easily accessible and a key part of Boston's vibrant cultural scene. The surrounding area offers a variety of dining and entertainment options, making it a perfect destination for a night out in the city.

The theater's rich history, elegant design, and diverse programming continue to attract a wide range of audiences. Whether attending a comedy show, a concert, or a theatrical production, visitors to the Wilbur Theatre are sure to enjoy a memorable and engaging experience in one of Boston's most cherished venues.

Boston Symphony Hall

Boston Symphony Hall, located on Massachusetts Avenue, is home to the Boston Symphony Orchestra (BSO) and is widely regarded as one of the world's greatest concert halls. Opened in 1900, Symphony Hall was designed by architects McKim, Mead & White in collaboration with Wallace Clement Sabine, a pioneer in architectural acoustics. The hall was constructed with the goal of achieving the best possible acoustics, and its design is based on the principles of a "shoebox" shape, which is ideal for concert sound.

Symphony Hall's interior is an elegant blend of classical and Renaissance styles, featuring a coffered ceiling, Greek and Roman statuary, and ornate details that enhance both its visual and acoustic appeal. The stage is set within a proscenium arch and is surrounded by tiers of seating that provide excellent sightlines and sound distribution.

The hall has been the home of the Boston Symphony Orchestra since its opening, and it also hosts performances by the Boston Pops Orchestra, founded by Arthur Fiedler. The BSO, under the direction of numerous distinguished conductors such as Serge Koussevitzky, Seiji Ozawa, and Andris Nelsons, has established itself as one of the leading orchestras in the world, renowned for its exceptional artistry and diverse repertoire.

Symphony Hall's acoustics are legendary, with critics and musicians alike praising its clear, warm, and balanced sound. The hall has seen countless memorable performances, including world premieres of significant works by composers like Igor Stravinsky, Aaron Copland, and Leonard Bernstein.

In addition to orchestral concerts, Symphony Hall hosts a variety of events, including chamber music performances, lectures, and community programs. The venue's commitment to education is evident in its outreach initiatives, which aim to make classical music accessible to a broader audience, particularly young people.

Boston Symphony Hall is a cultural treasure that offers an unparalleled concert experience. Whether attending a BSO performance, a Boston Pops concert, or a special event, visitors are sure to be captivated by the hall's stunning acoustics, architectural beauty, and the high caliber of its performances.

Charles Playhouse

The Charles Playhouse, located in Boston's Theatre District on Warrenton Street, is a historic venue known for its intimate setting and its eclectic programming. Originally built as a church in 1839, the building was converted into a theater in the 1950s and has since become a beloved institution in the city's vibrant arts scene.

The Playhouse has a rich history of presenting innovative and diverse performances. In the 1960s, it was a hub for Boston's burgeoning experimental theater movement, showcasing works by emerging playwrights and avant-garde productions. Over the years, the Charles Playhouse has evolved to host a wide range of performances, from traditional plays and musicals to cutting-edge contemporary shows.

Today, the Charles Playhouse is best known as the long-running home of two highly popular and unique shows: Blue Man Group and Shear Madness. Blue Man Group, an avant-garde performance art troupe known for its energetic, multimedia performances, has been a staple at the Playhouse since 1995. The show combines music, comedy, and multimedia theatrics to create a one-of-a-kind entertainment experience that appeals to audiences of all ages.

Shear Madness, an interactive murder mystery comedy, has been running at the Charles Playhouse since 1980. The show's format allows the audience to participate in solving the crime, making each performance unique. Its blend of humor, improvisation, and audience involvement has made it one of the longest-running non-musical plays in American theater history.

The Charles Playhouse's cozy and welcoming atmosphere, with seating for just under 500 patrons, provides an intimate theater experience where audiences can feel closely connected to the performers. The venue's commitment to innovative programming and its ability to adapt to the changing tastes of theatergoers have ensured its enduring popularity.

Whether you're attending a groundbreaking performance by Blue Man Group, enjoying the comedic twists of Shear Madness, or catching another engaging production, the Charles Playhouse offers a memorable and distinctive theater experience in the heart of Boston.

Huntington Theatre

The Huntington Theatre, located on the Avenue of the Arts (Huntington Avenue), is one of Boston's premier cultural institutions, renowned for its high-quality productions and commitment to theatrical excellence. Founded in 1982, the Huntington Theatre Company has established itself as a leading force in the American theater scene, garnering numerous awards, including the prestigious Regional Theatre Tony Award in 2013.

The theater itself is a historic venue, originally built in 1925 as part of Boston University's College of Fine Arts. Its grand architecture and elegant interior create a sophisticated setting that enhances the theatergoing experience. The venue includes the 890-seat mainstage and the smaller, more intimate Calderwood Pavilion at the Boston Center for the Arts, which hosts the company's new works and experimental productions.

The Huntington Theatre Company is known for its diverse repertoire, which includes classic plays, contemporary works, and world premieres. The company has a strong tradition of nurturing new talent and developing new plays, often working with playwrights, directors, and designers to bring fresh and innovative productions to the stage.

The Huntington's commitment to education and community engagement is reflected in its extensive outreach programs. These include student matinees, in-school residencies, and workshops designed to make theater accessible to young people and foster a love of the arts. The company also offers a robust internship and fellowship program that provides training and professional development opportunities for aspiring theater professionals.

In addition to its regular season of productions, the Huntington Theatre Company hosts various special events, including panel discussions, lectures, and behind-the-scenes tours that offer audiences deeper insights into the creative process and the themes explored in the plays.

The Huntington Theatre's reputation for excellence, its commitment to new work, and its dedication to community engagement make it a cornerstone of Boston's cultural landscape. Whether attending a classic production, a contemporary play, or a groundbreaking new work, visitors to the Huntington Theatre can expect a thought-provoking and enriching theatrical experience.

Shubert Theatre

The Shubert Theatre, located on Tremont Street in Boston's Theatre District, is a historic venue known for its elegant architecture and rich legacy of theatrical performances. Opened in 1910, the Shubert Theatre was designed by the renowned architectural firm of Herts & Tallant and has been a key player in Boston's cultural scene for over a century.

The Shubert Theatre's design is a beautiful example of early 20th-century theater architecture, featuring a classical façade, ornate detailing, and a lavish interior with plush seating, crystal chandeliers, and intricate moldings. The theater's intimate atmosphere, with a seating capacity of approximately 1,500, provides audiences with a close and personal connection to the performances on stage.

Throughout its history, the Shubert Theatre has hosted a wide variety of performances, including Broadway shows, operas, ballets, concerts, and more. It has been the venue for many notable productions and performers, contributing to its reputation as one of Boston's premier theaters.

The Shubert Theatre is part of the Boch Center, a non-profit organization that manages several of Boston's historic theaters and promotes arts education and community engagement. As a member of the Boch Center, the Shubert Theatre benefits from a commitment to preserving its historic character while ensuring it remains a vibrant and active part of the city's cultural life.

The theater's programming includes touring Broadway productions, concerts by renowned musicians, dance performances, and family-friendly shows. This diverse lineup ensures that there is something for everyone, appealing to a wide range of tastes and interests.

In addition to its regular performances, the Shubert Theatre hosts various educational programs and community events. These initiatives aim to make the arts accessible to a broader audience, particularly young people, and to foster a greater appreciation for the performing arts.

The Shubert Theatre's blend of historic charm, architectural beauty, and diverse programming make it a cherished cultural landmark in Boston. Whether attending a Broadway hit, a classical concert, or a special event, visitors to the Shubert Theatre are sure to enjoy a memorable and enriching experience in one of the city's most iconic venues.

Historic Sites

Freedom Trail

The Freedom Trail is a 2.5-mile-long path through downtown Boston that connects 16 significant historical sites, offering a rich tapestry of the city's and the nation's early history. Established in 1951, the Freedom Trail guides visitors through the heart of Boston, providing an immersive experience of the American Revolution and its legacy.

Marked by a red brick or painted line, the trail begins at Boston Common, the oldest public park in the United States, and winds its way to the Bunker Hill Monument in Charlestown. Along the way, it passes iconic landmarks such as the Massachusetts State House, Paul Revere's House, and the USS Constitution, each site contributing to the narrative of America's fight for independence.

One of the trail's key features is its accessibility and self-guided nature, allowing visitors to explore at their own pace. Numerous guided tours are also available, providing expert insights into the historical significance of each site and the broader context of the Revolutionary era.

The Freedom Trail is not only a journey through history but also a showcase of Boston's architectural and cultural heritage. It highlights a variety of structures, from colonial-era buildings to Victorian masterpieces, reflecting the city's evolution over the centuries.

Educational programs and reenactments along the trail bring history to life, offering interactive experiences for visitors of all ages. These programs aim to deepen understanding and appreciation of the events and individuals who played pivotal roles in America's quest for freedom.

Whether you're a history enthusiast, a student, or a curious traveler, the Freedom Trail offers a unique and enriching way to explore Boston. It stands as a testament to the city's pivotal role in the birth of the United States, inviting all who walk its path to connect with the foundational stories of the American nation.

Old State House

The Old State House, located at the intersection of Washington and State Streets in Boston, is one of the city's oldest and most historically significant buildings. Constructed in 1713, it served as the seat of colonial and state government and played a central role in the events leading up to the American Revolution.

The building's architecture is a striking example of Georgian style, characterized by its brick façade, elegant proportions, and intricate detailing. The Old State House's balcony is particularly notable, as it was from here that the Declaration of Independence was first read to the people of Boston on July 18, 1776.

Inside, the Old State House has been meticulously preserved and restored to reflect its historical significance. It now operates as a museum, managed by the Bostonian Society, offering a wealth of exhibits and artifacts that tell the story of Boston's colonial past and the birth of American democracy.

The museum's exhibits cover a range of topics, from the daily lives of Bostonians in the 18th century to the pivotal events of the Revolutionary period. Highlights include displays on the Boston Massacre, which took place just outside the building in 1770, and the subsequent trial, where John Adams famously defended the British soldiers involved.

Visitors can explore the Council Chamber, where the Royal Governor and his council met, and the Representatives Hall, where debates on liberty and governance took place. These rooms are filled with period furnishings and artifacts that provide a vivid picture of colonial government and society.

The Old State House is a key stop on Boston's Freedom Trail, attracting history enthusiasts, students, and tourists from around the world. Its central location and historical significance make it an essential destination for anyone interested in the origins of American independence.

Whether you're delving into the detailed exhibits or simply admiring the building's architectural beauty, a visit to the Old State House offers a profound connection to the early history of Boston and the United States.

Old South Meeting House

The Old South Meeting House, located on the corner of Washington and Milk Streets in Boston, is a historic landmark that played a crucial role in the events leading up to the American Revolution. Built in 1729 as a Puritan meeting house, it quickly became a center for both religious worship and political discourse.

The building's architecture is a fine example of colonial New England meeting house design, featuring a simple yet elegant exterior with a prominent steeple. Inside, the spacious hall, with its high ceiling and tall windows, was designed to accommodate large gatherings, making it an ideal venue for public meetings and debates.

The Old South Meeting House is most famous for its role in the Boston Tea Party. On December 16, 1773, over 5,000 colonists gathered here to protest the British Tea Act, which had imposed taxes on tea without colonial representation. The impassioned speeches and heated discussions that took place within its walls led directly to the decision to dump 342 chests of British tea into Boston Harbor, an act of defiance that became a pivotal moment in the American Revolution.

Today, the Old South Meeting House operates as a museum and historic site, preserving the legacy of its revolutionary past. Exhibits within the museum explore the events leading up to the Boston Tea Party, the building's role in colonial Boston, and its continued significance as a symbol of free speech and assembly.

Visitors can see artifacts from the period, including tea leaves from the Boston Tea Party, as well as original furnishings and architectural features that have been carefully preserved. The museum also offers educational programs, lectures, and reenactments that bring history to life for visitors of all ages.

The Old South Meeting House is an essential stop on the Freedom Trail, offering a profound connection to the ideas and actions that sparked the American Revolution. Its rich history and enduring legacy make it a must-visit destination for anyone interested in the origins of American independence and the power of collective action.

Whether you're exploring the exhibits, participating in a reenactment, or simply reflecting on the events that unfolded within its walls, a visit to the Old South Meeting House provides a powerful and immersive experience of Boston's revolutionary past.

King's Chapel

King's Chapel, located at the corner of Tremont and School Streets in downtown Boston, is a historic church known for its architectural beauty and rich history. Founded in 1686 as the first Anglican church in New England, King's Chapel played a significant role in the religious and cultural life of colonial Boston.

The original wooden church was replaced by the current stone structure in 1754, designed by architect Peter Harrison. This building is a stunning example of Georgian architecture, featuring a grand façade with tall columns and a prominent bell tower. The interior is equally impressive, with elegant wooden pews, a high pulpit, and a beautiful organ that dates back to 1756.

King's Chapel has been at the center of many important events in Boston's history. During the American Revolution, the church was a focal point of Loyalist activity. After the Revolution, it became the first Unitarian church in America under the leadership of James Freeman, who reinterpreted the Anglican liturgy to align with Unitarian beliefs.

Today, King's Chapel is both an active house of worship and a historic site. Visitors can attend services, concerts, and special events, as well as take guided tours that explore the church's architecture, history, and the crypts below, where notable Bostonians are buried.

The adjacent King's Chapel Burying Ground, established in 1630, is the oldest burial ground in Boston and the final resting place of many early settlers, including Mary Chilton, a Mayflower passenger, and John Winthrop, the first governor of Massachusetts Bay Colony.

King's Chapel continues to be a symbol of Boston's rich religious and historical heritage, offering a serene and contemplative space amidst the bustling city. Whether you're interested in its architectural splendor, its historical significance, or its ongoing spiritual life, a visit to King's Chapel provides a deep connection to Boston's past.

Granary Burying Ground

The Granary Burying Ground, located on Tremont Street in Boston, is one of the city's oldest and most significant cemeteries. Established in 1660, it is the final resting place of many notable figures from the colonial and

Revolutionary periods, making it a vital landmark for those interested in American history.

The cemetery's name derives from an adjacent grain storage building that once stood nearby. Covering roughly two acres, the Granary Burying Ground features rows of weathered tombstones and elaborate monuments that provide a glimpse into the 17th and 18th centuries.

Among the prominent individuals buried here are three signers of the Declaration of Independence: John Hancock, Samuel Adams, and Robert Treat Paine. Hancock's grave is marked by a grand obelisk, while Adams' and Paine's graves are more modest but equally significant.

Another notable grave is that of Paul Revere, the famous patriot known for his midnight ride. Revere's tombstone is one of the most visited sites in the cemetery, drawing countless visitors who wish to pay their respects to this iconic American figure.

The Granary Burying Ground is also the final resting place of victims of the Boston Massacre, including Crispus Attucks, whose grave is marked by a memorial. Additionally, the cemetery contains the graves of other influential colonial leaders, such as James Otis and Peter Faneuil.

Walking through the Granary Burying Ground, visitors can reflect on the lives and contributions of those who helped shape the early history of the United States. The cemetery's serene atmosphere and historical markers provide a poignant reminder of the nation's past.

As part of the Freedom Trail, the Granary Burying Ground is an essential stop for anyone exploring Boston's historical sites. Its well-preserved graves and informative plaques offer a unique opportunity to connect with the city's colonial heritage and the individuals who played pivotal roles in America's founding.

Boston Massacre Site

The Boston Massacre Site, located in front of the Old State House at the intersection of Congress and State Streets, is a pivotal landmark in American history. On March 5, 1770, this site was the scene of a deadly confrontation between British soldiers and American colonists, an event that significantly escalated tensions leading up to the American Revolution.

The incident began when a crowd of colonists gathered to protest the presence of British troops in Boston, which had been stationed in the city to enforce unpopular taxation laws. As the crowd grew more hostile, the soldiers fired into the crowd, killing five colonists and wounding several others. Among the victims were Crispus Attucks, Samuel Gray, James Caldwell, Samuel Maverick, and Patrick Carr.

The Boston Massacre quickly became a symbol of British tyranny and colonial resistance. The event was widely publicized by patriot leaders such as Samuel Adams and Paul Revere, whose famous engraving of the incident helped galvanize public opinion against British rule. The soldiers involved were later tried for murder, with future president John Adams serving as their defense attorney, arguing for fair trial principles despite his personal patriot sympathies.

Today, the Boston Massacre Site is marked by a circular cobblestone pattern in the pavement, commemorating the location where the tragic event took place. Visitors to the site can reflect on the significance of the massacre and its role in the broader context of the American struggle for independence.

The nearby Old State House, which now houses a museum, offers exhibits and artifacts related to the Boston Massacre and the events leading up to the Revolution. Visitors can explore the balcony where the Declaration of Independence was first read to Bostonians and view the courtroom where the soldiers were tried.

As part of the Freedom Trail, the Boston Massacre Site is an essential stop for anyone interested in the origins of the American Revolution. It provides a tangible connection to the past and a reminder of the sacrifices made in the pursuit of liberty and justice.

Fort Warren (Boston Harbor Islands)

Fort Warren, located on Georges Island in the Boston Harbor Islands National and State Park, is a historic fortification that played a significant role in American military history. Constructed between 1833 and 1861, Fort Warren was designed to protect Boston Harbor and its vital shipping lanes from potential naval attacks. The fort is named after Dr. Joseph Warren, a patriot killed in the Battle of Bunker Hill.

Built with granite and brick, Fort Warren is an impressive example of 19th-century military architecture. The fort features a star-shaped design with bastions, gun emplacements, and thick walls capable of withstanding heavy bombardment. During the Civil War, Fort Warren served as a training ground for Union soldiers and a prison for Confederate officers and political prisoners, including Confederate Vice President Alexander H. Stephens.

Today, Fort Warren is a popular destination for history enthusiasts and outdoor adventurers alike. Visitors can explore the well-preserved fortifications, tour the prison cells, and view the various cannons and other military artifacts on display. The fort offers guided tours that provide insights into its history, construction, and the daily lives of those who served or were imprisoned there.

The island itself is part of the Boston Harbor Islands National and State Park, which includes 34 islands and peninsulas. Georges Island offers scenic views of the harbor and the Boston skyline, making it a perfect spot for picnicking, hiking, and birdwatching. Seasonal ferry service provides easy access to the island from downtown Boston.

Fort Warren and Georges Island offer a unique blend of historical intrigue and natural beauty, providing visitors with a chance to step back in time and enjoy the great outdoors. Whether you're exploring the fort's dark corridors, learning about its strategic importance, or simply enjoying a peaceful day by the water, a visit to Fort Warren is a rewarding experience.

Dorchester Heights

Dorchester Heights, located in South Boston, is a historic site that played a pivotal role in the American Revolutionary War. It was here, in March 1776, that General George Washington's Continental Army fortified the heights with cannons captured from Fort Ticonderoga, forcing the British to evacuate Boston.

The dramatic events at Dorchester Heights marked a significant turning point in the war. Using the strategic high ground, Washington's forces positioned artillery that threatened the British fleet in Boston Harbor and their fortifications in the city. Faced with this new threat, British General William Howe decided to withdraw his troops, effectively ending the Siege of Boston and giving the Continental Army a crucial early victory.

Today, Dorchester Heights is commemorated by the Dorchester Heights Monument, a white marble Georgian Revival tower built in 1902. The monument stands as a tribute to the strategic ingenuity and determination of Washington and his troops. The surrounding park offers sweeping views of Boston and its harbor, providing a scenic and contemplative setting for visitors.

The park is part of the Boston National Historical Park and offers interpretive signs that provide historical context about the siege and the fortification of Dorchester Heights. It is a popular spot for history enthusiasts, locals, and tourists who come to appreciate the significance of the site and its role in securing American independence.

Dorchester Heights also hosts various events and reenactments that bring the history of the American Revolution to life. These activities, along with the monument and the park's natural beauty, make it a compelling destination for anyone interested in the early struggles of the United States.

Whether you're a history buff, a local resident, or a visitor to Boston, Dorchester Heights offers a unique glimpse into the past and an opportunity to reflect on the courage and resilience of the Continental Army. The site stands as a testament to the strategic brilliance of George Washington and the pivotal moments that shaped the nation's fight for independence.

Plimoth Plantation (near Boston)

Plimoth Plantation, located in Plymouth, Massachusetts, about 40 miles south of Boston, is a living history museum that brings to life the early days of the Plymouth Colony, one of the first successful English settlements in North America. Established in 1947, the museum provides a comprehensive and immersive experience of 17th-century colonial and Native American life.

The museum features meticulously recreated environments, including the 1627 English Village, a detailed reconstruction of the Pilgrims' settlement. Costumed interpreters, portraying actual residents of the colony, engage with visitors in character, sharing stories of their daily lives, struggles, and triumphs. This interactive approach allows visitors to gain a deeper understanding of the challenges faced by the early settlers and their interactions with the Native Wampanoag people.

Adjacent to the English Village is the Wampanoag Homesite, which represents the life of the Indigenous people who lived in the region long before the arrival of the Pilgrims. Native interpreters, who are members of

Indigenous nations, provide insights into Wampanoag culture, traditions, and history, offering a balanced perspective on the early colonial period.

The museum also includes the Craft Center, where artisans demonstrate traditional crafts such as pottery, woodworking, and textile production, using techniques from the 17th century. Visitors can learn about the skills and trades that were essential to the survival and prosperity of the colony.

In addition to its historical reenactments and demonstrations, Plimoth Plantation offers educational programs, workshops, and special events that delve deeper into the history and heritage of the early settlers and Native Americans. Seasonal events, such as the Thanksgiving celebrations, provide a unique opportunity to experience historical traditions and cultural practices.

Plimoth Plantation also manages the Mayflower II, a full-scale reproduction of the ship that brought the Pilgrims to America in 1620. The ship is docked at Plymouth Harbor and is open for tours, giving visitors a sense of the arduous journey undertaken by the Pilgrims.

A visit to Plimoth Plantation offers a rich, educational experience that brings history to life in a vivid and engaging way. It provides a profound understanding of the early interactions between the Pilgrims and the Wampanoag people, highlighting the complexities and challenges of 17th-century colonial life.

Minute Man National Historical Park (near Boston)

Minute Man National Historical Park, located in Concord, Lexington, and Lincoln, Massachusetts, preserves and interprets the sites and events associated with the opening battles of the American Revolutionary War on April 19, 1775. This park offers a rich historical experience, allowing visitors to explore the landscapes where the first shots of the Revolution were fired.

The park encompasses several key sites along the 5-mile Battle Road Trail, which follows the route taken by British troops as they marched from Boston to Concord and back. The trail is lined with historic landmarks, reconstructed colonial homes, and informative exhibits that provide insights into the events of that fateful day.

One of the highlights of the park is the North Bridge in Concord, where the "shot heard 'round the world" was fired. This site marks the location of the first major conflict between the British soldiers and the colonial militia. A visit to the North Bridge includes the Minute Man Statue, an iconic symbol of the patriot fight for independence, and the North Bridge Visitor Center, which offers exhibits and interpretive programs about the battle and its significance.

The park also features the Hartwell Tavern, a restored 18th-century tavern that served as a gathering place for patriots during the Revolution. Costumed interpreters provide demonstrations and reenactments, bringing the period to life for visitors.

Another key site is the Lexington Battle Green, where the first shots of the Revolutionary War were fired at dawn. The green is home to several monuments and memorials, including the Lexington Minuteman Statue and the Old Belfry. The nearby Hancock-Clarke House, which served as a refuge for John Hancock and Samuel Adams, offers additional historical context and exhibits.

Minute Man National Historical Park provides a variety of educational programs, guided tours, and special events that commemorate the early struggles for American independence. The park's rangers and volunteers offer insights into the lives of the colonial militia and the strategic importance of the battles fought on this ground.

The park's scenic landscapes, historic sites, and well-preserved trails offer a unique opportunity to explore the birthplace of the American Revolution. Whether you're a history enthusiast, a student, or a casual visitor, Minute Man National Historical Park provides a profound connection to the nation's fight for freedom and the individuals who played pivotal roles in its founding.

Observation Decks

Skywalk Observatory at the Prudential Center

The Skywalk Observatory at the Prudential Center offers one of the most spectacular views of Boston. Located on the 50th floor of the Prudential Tower, the Skywalk Observatory provides a 360-degree panoramic view of the city and beyond, stretching up to 100 miles on a clear day. Opened in 1964, the Prudential Tower, often referred to as "The Pru," is one of the tallest buildings in Boston, standing at 749 feet.

The observatory not only offers breathtaking vistas but also serves as an educational experience with its interactive exhibits. The Dreams of Freedom Museum, located within the Skywalk, provides insights into Boston's rich history of immigration, showcasing the diverse cultural influences that have shaped the city. Audio tours, available in multiple languages, guide visitors through the significant landmarks visible from the observatory, enhancing the experience with historical and cultural context.

Visitors can spot many of Boston's iconic sites from the Skywalk, including Fenway Park, the Charles River, the Boston Common, and the State House with its distinctive golden dome. The observatory also offers stunning views of the surrounding New England landscape, including the Atlantic Ocean and the distant White Mountains.

The Skywalk Observatory is an ideal destination for both tourists and locals, providing a unique perspective of Boston's skyline. Whether you're learning about the city's history, identifying landmarks, or simply enjoying the view, the Skywalk Observatory offers a memorable experience high above the bustling city streets.

Custom House Tower Observation Deck

The Custom House Tower, located in the heart of downtown Boston, is one of the city's most recognizable landmarks. Originally built in 1847 as a Greek Revival-style custom house, the structure was transformed in 1915 with the addition of a 496-foot clock tower, making it Boston's first skyscraper at the time. Today, the Custom House Tower is a luxury hotel, but its 26th-floor observation deck remains a popular attraction for visitors seeking panoramic views of the city.

The observation deck offers a stunning 360-degree perspective of Boston, including views of the Boston Harbor, the North End, and the financial district. On a clear day, visitors can see as far as the Blue Hills and other surrounding landscapes, making it a perfect spot for photography and sightseeing.

Access to the observation deck is available through guided tours, which provide not only breathtaking views but also historical context about the Custom House and its significance in Boston's development. The guides share fascinating stories about the building's architectural evolution, its role in maritime trade, and its transformation into a hotel.

The Custom House Tower's clock, a prominent feature of the Boston skyline, is an impressive sight from the observation deck. The large clock faces add a unique charm to the viewing experience, and the tower's design offers a blend of historical elegance and modern sophistication.

In addition to the observation deck, the Custom House Tower features a beautiful rotunda with intricate mosaics and marble floors, showcasing the building's architectural grandeur. The building's lobby and lower levels also provide a glimpse into its storied past, with historical exhibits and artwork.

The Custom House Tower Observation Deck is a must-visit for anyone looking to experience Boston from above. Its combination of historical significance, architectural beauty, and sweeping views make it a standout destination in the city. Whether you're a history enthusiast, a photography buff, or simply in search of a unique vantage point, the Custom House Tower offers an unforgettable experience high above the bustling streets of Boston.

Neighborhood Exploration

Beacon Hill

Beacon Hill is one of Boston's most picturesque and historic neighborhoods, known for its charming, narrow streets, brick sidewalks, and gaslit street lamps. Located just north of the Boston Common and the Massachusetts State House, Beacon Hill is a symbol of Boston's rich history and colonial heritage.

The neighborhood is named for the beacon that once stood atop its highest point, which was used to warn residents of an invasion. Today, Beacon Hill is a designated National Historic Landmark District, preserving its 19th-century architecture and historical significance.

Beacon Hill's architecture is characterized by Federal-style row houses, many of which date back to the early 1800s. The area is home to some of the city's most notable historic sites, including the Massachusetts State House with its iconic golden dome, which overlooks the Boston Common.

Acorn Street, one of the most photographed streets in America, epitomizes the neighborhood's historic charm with its cobblestone pavement and beautifully preserved homes. Louisburg Square, a private square lined with elegant townhouses, has been home to many prominent Bostonians, including the novelist Louisa May Alcott.

Beacon Hill is not only a residential area but also a cultural hub. The Boston Athenaeum, one of the oldest independent libraries in the United States, offers a rich collection of books and art. The neighborhood is also home to the Museum of African American History, which celebrates the legacy of Boston's African American community and includes the historic African Meeting House.

Charles Street, the main thoroughfare, is lined with boutique shops, antique stores, cafes, and restaurants, providing a vibrant commercial area that complements the residential streets. This blend of history, culture, and modern amenities makes Beacon Hill a unique and desirable place to live and visit.

Whether you're strolling along its charming streets, exploring its historic sites, or enjoying the local shops and eateries, Beacon Hill offers a quintessential Boston experience that highlights the city's colonial past and its continued vibrancy.

North End (Little Italy)

The North End, also known as Boston's Little Italy, is a vibrant and historic neighborhood renowned for its rich cultural heritage and delicious Italian cuisine. Located along the waterfront and adjacent to the Financial District, the North End is one of Boston's oldest residential communities, dating back to the 1630s.

The neighborhood is characterized by its narrow, winding streets and a mix of old and new architecture, reflecting its long history and ongoing vitality. The North End is home to several significant historical sites, including the Paul Revere House, the oldest building in downtown Boston, and the Old North Church, famous for its role in Paul Revere's midnight ride.

The North End's Italian heritage is its most defining feature, evident in the numerous Italian restaurants, bakeries, cafes, and specialty food shops that line its streets. Hanover Street, the main artery of the neighborhood, is bustling with diners and shoppers enjoying authentic Italian dishes, pastries, and espresso. Iconic establishments like Mike's Pastry, Modern Pastry, and Regina Pizzeria are must-visit destinations for both locals and tourists.

In addition to its culinary delights, the North End hosts several annual cultural and religious festivals that draw large crowds. The Feast of St. Anthony and the Feast of St. Agrippina are among the most famous, featuring parades, music, food stalls, and religious processions that celebrate the neighborhood's Italian roots and community spirit.

The North End's waterfront location also adds to its charm, offering scenic views of Boston Harbor and easy access to the Harborwalk, a public walkway that stretches along the waterfront. The neighborhood's close-knit community, vibrant atmosphere, and historical significance make it a beloved part of Boston.

Whether you're exploring its historic landmarks, savoring its culinary offerings, or participating in its lively festivals, the North End provides a rich and immersive experience that captures the essence of Boston's cultural diversity and historical depth.

Back Bay

Back Bay is one of Boston's most upscale and architecturally significant neighborhoods, known for its Victorian brownstone homes, tree-lined streets, and notable landmarks. Developed in the mid-19th century on reclaimed land from the Charles River, Back Bay is a masterful example of urban planning and design.

The neighborhood is bounded by the Charles River Esplanade to the north, the Boston Public Garden to the east, and stretches westward to Kenmore Square. Its grid-like street layout and European-style avenues, such as Commonwealth Avenue, showcase the neighborhood's elegant and orderly design.

Back Bay is home to several iconic landmarks and institutions. The Boston Public Library, located in Copley Square, is a masterpiece of Renaissance Revival architecture and houses an extensive collection of books and art. Trinity Church, also in Copley Square, is an architectural gem known for its Richardsonian Romanesque style and stunning stained-glass windows.

Newbury Street, often referred to as Boston's premier shopping destination, runs parallel to Commonwealth Avenue and is lined with high-end boutiques, art galleries, cafes, and restaurants. The street's blend of historic charm and modern luxury makes it a popular spot for both locals and visitors.

The John Hancock Tower, Boston's tallest building, and the Prudential Center, with its Skywalk Observatory and shopping complex, add a modern skyline to the neighborhood's historic backdrop. The Prudential Center also houses the Top of the Hub restaurant, offering panoramic views of the city.

Back Bay's proximity to the Charles River Esplanade provides residents and visitors with beautiful green spaces for walking, jogging, and cycling along the river. The Esplanade also hosts various events and concerts, particularly during the summer months.

Residential life in Back Bay is characterized by elegant brownstone homes and luxury apartments, offering a blend of historical ambiance and modern amenities. The neighborhood's excellent public transportation links, including multiple subway lines and bus routes, make it an accessible and convenient place to live.

Back Bay's combination of architectural beauty, cultural landmarks, and vibrant commercial areas make it one of Boston's most desirable neighborhoods. Whether you're exploring its historic streets, shopping on Newbury Street, or enjoying the riverfront, Back Bay offers a rich and diverse urban experience.

South End

The South End is one of Boston's most vibrant and diverse neighborhoods, known for its Victorian brownstone buildings, tree-lined streets, and lively arts scene. Developed in the mid-19th century, the South End was designed with broad avenues and picturesque parks, creating a charming and accessible urban environment. It is listed on the National Register of Historic Places, recognized for its architectural significance and well-preserved row houses.

Tremont Street, Columbus Avenue, and Washington Street are the neighborhood's main thoroughfares, bustling with a mix of trendy restaurants, boutique shops, and art galleries. The South End is particularly renowned for its dining scene, offering a wide range of culinary experiences from casual cafes to fine dining establishments. Popular spots include Toro, a Spanish tapas bar, and Myers + Chang, an Asian fusion restaurant.

The South End is also a cultural hub, home to numerous art galleries and studios, many of which participate in the monthly First Fridays event, where galleries open their doors to the public for art viewings and receptions. The Boston Center for the Arts (BCA) is a cornerstone of the neighborhood's cultural life, hosting theater productions, art exhibitions, and community events. The BCA's Calderwood Pavilion and the Cyclorama are notable venues that support a wide array of performances and visual arts.

Parks and green spaces, such as the South End's network of community gardens and the beautiful Blackstone and Franklin Squares, provide residents and visitors with tranquil spots to relax and enjoy the outdoors. These green spaces contribute to the neighborhood's reputation as one of Boston's most liveable and attractive areas.

The South End's diverse population, which includes artists, young professionals, families, and a vibrant LGBTQ+ community, adds to its dynamic and welcoming atmosphere. The neighborhood hosts several annual events, such as the South End Open Studios, the SoWa Art + Design District's markets, and the South End Garden Tour, all of which showcase the community's creativity and engagement.

With its blend of historic charm, cultural richness, and modern amenities, the South End is a distinctive and appealing destination within Boston, offering something for everyone to enjoy.

Cambridge (Harvard Square)

Harvard Square, located in Cambridge, Massachusetts, is a historic and bustling epicenter of intellectual and cultural activity, primarily known for its association with Harvard University. Situated just across the Charles River from Boston, Harvard Square is easily accessible and serves as a major hub for students, academics, and tourists.

The area around Harvard Square is steeped in history, with Harvard University, founded in 1636, being one of the oldest and most prestigious institutions of higher education in the United States. The university's historic campus, with its ivy-covered buildings and stately quads, provides a picturesque backdrop for the lively square.

Harvard Square itself is a vibrant mix of shops, cafes, bookstores, and cultural venues. The Harvard Book Store and the Coop (Harvard Cooperative Society) are must-visit destinations for book lovers, offering a wide selection of titles and a cozy atmosphere. The square also features an array of dining options, from casual eateries and coffee shops to fine dining restaurants. Popular spots include Grendel's Den, a long-standing pub, and Alden & Harlow, known for its innovative American cuisine.

Cultural institutions abound in Harvard Square. The Harvard Art Museums house an impressive collection of art from around the world, while the American Repertory Theater (A.R.T.) is renowned for its cutting-edge productions and world premieres. Additionally, the Brattle Theatre is a beloved independent cinema that screens classic, foreign, and indie films.

Harvard Yard, the historic center of Harvard University, is open to the public and offers a tranquil place to stroll and soak in the academic atmosphere. The yard is surrounded by notable buildings such as the Widener Library, Memorial Church, and Massachusetts Hall.

Harvard Square is also a hub for street performers, festivals, and public events, adding to its dynamic and engaging environment. The annual MayFair and Oktoberfest celebrations draw large crowds with their lively music, food stalls, and entertainment.

Whether exploring its academic institutions, enjoying its diverse culinary scene, or participating in its cultural events, Harvard Square offers a rich and multifaceted experience that reflects the vibrant spirit of Cambridge and its historic ties to higher learning and culture.

Seaport District

The Seaport District, also known as the South Boston Waterfront, is one of Boston's most rapidly developing and dynamic neighborhoods. Located along the city's waterfront, the Seaport District has transformed from a bustling maritime hub into a modern urban enclave known for its sleek architecture, innovative businesses, and vibrant cultural scene.

The district's revitalization began in the early 2000s, and today it boasts a mix of high-end residential buildings, cutting-edge office spaces, and a wide array of entertainment and dining options. The waterfront area provides stunning views of Boston Harbor and offers numerous outdoor activities, including harbor walks, public art installations, and parks.

The Seaport District is home to the Boston Convention and Exhibition Center (BCEC), one of the largest convention centers in the Northeast, attracting a wide range of conferences, trade shows, and events. The nearby Institute of Contemporary Art (ICA) is a cultural landmark in the district, featuring contemporary art exhibitions, performances, and an architecturally striking building that extends over the harbor.

Dining in the Seaport District is a culinary adventure, with an impressive array of restaurants and bars offering diverse cuisines and waterfront views. Notable dining destinations include Legal Harborside, a multi-level seafood restaurant, and The Barking Crab, a casual spot known for its fresh seafood and lively atmosphere. The district also boasts trendy rooftop bars and craft breweries, such as Harpoon Brewery, which offers tours and tastings.

Retail options in the Seaport District have expanded significantly, with the opening of Seaport Square, a mixed-use development that includes shopping, dining, and entertainment venues. The district's retail landscape features everything from high-end boutiques to popular chain stores, catering to a variety of shopping preferences.

The Seaport District is also known for its innovative business environment, housing numerous tech startups, biotech firms, and global companies. The neighborhood's modern infrastructure and proximity to Boston's financial district make it an attractive location for businesses and professionals.

With its combination of scenic waterfront views, cultural attractions, culinary delights, and thriving business community, the Seaport District offers a unique and exciting experience for residents and visitors alike. Whether exploring its museums, enjoying its dining options, or taking in the harbor views, the Seaport District represents the future of Boston's urban development.

Charlestown

Charlestown is a historic and picturesque neighborhood located just across the Charles River from downtown Boston. Established in 1628, it is one of the oldest neighborhoods in Boston and is rich in colonial and Revolutionary War history. The neighborhood's charming streets, lined with brick row houses and historic landmarks, reflect its deep-rooted past and vibrant community spirit.

One of Charlestown's most famous landmarks is the Bunker Hill Monument, a towering granite obelisk commemorating the Battle of Bunker Hill, one of the first major conflicts of the American Revolutionary War. Visitors can climb the 294 steps to the top for panoramic views of Boston and its harbor. The nearby Bunker Hill Museum provides additional context and exhibits related to the battle and the broader Revolutionary period.

The USS Constitution, also known as "Old Ironsides," is another iconic attraction in Charlestown. This historic naval vessel, launched in 1797, is the oldest commissioned warship afloat in the world. It is docked at the Charlestown Navy Yard, where visitors can tour the ship and learn about its storied past at the accompanying museum.

Charlestown's residential areas are known for their well-preserved Federal-style and Victorian homes, many of which date back to the 18th and 19th centuries. The neighborhood's tight-knit community and historic charm make it a desirable place to live. The streets of Charlestown are often bustling with activity, particularly around the local shops, cafes, and restaurants that give the area its distinctive character.

The neighborhood also features several parks and green spaces, including the scenic Paul Revere Park and the Charlestown Navy Yard Park, which offer recreational opportunities and stunning views of the Boston skyline and waterfront.

Charlestown's mix of historical significance, architectural beauty, and community atmosphere make it a unique and appealing part of Boston. Whether exploring its historic sites, enjoying its waterfront, or strolling through its charming streets, visitors to Charlestown are sure to appreciate its rich heritage and welcoming environment.

Jamaica Plain

Jamaica Plain, often referred to as "JP" by locals, is a diverse and vibrant neighborhood located southwest of downtown Boston. Known for its strong sense of community, lush green spaces, and eclectic mix of residents, Jamaica Plain offers a unique blend of urban living and suburban tranquility.

One of the neighborhood's most defining features is its abundance of parks and green spaces. The Arnold Arboretum, a 281-acre botanical garden managed by Harvard University, is a jewel of Jamaica Plain. It offers a stunning array of plant species, beautifully landscaped grounds, and miles of walking paths, making it a favorite spot for nature lovers and outdoor enthusiasts.

Jamaica Pond, another popular destination, provides opportunities for boating, fishing, and picnicking. The 68-acre pond is surrounded by a picturesque park with walking and jogging trails, offering a peaceful retreat from the hustle and bustle of city life.

Centre Street, the main commercial thoroughfare in Jamaica Plain, is lined with a diverse array of shops, restaurants, cafes, and bars. The neighborhood is known for its strong support of local businesses and its vibrant cultural scene. From farm-to-table dining at spots like Ten Tables to craft beer at the local brewery, Turtle Swamp Brewing, there are plenty of culinary delights to explore.

Jamaica Plain is also home to a rich artistic community, with numerous galleries, studios, and performance spaces. The Jamaica Plain Arts Council organizes the annual Open Studios event, where local artists open their workspaces to the public, showcasing the neighborhood's creative talent.

The community's commitment to social justice and activism is another hallmark of Jamaica Plain. The neighborhood has a long history of civic engagement and is known for its inclusive and progressive values. Community gardens, farmers markets, and cooperative initiatives are common, reflecting the residents' dedication to sustainability and community building.

With its mix of historic homes, modern amenities, and a strong sense of community, Jamaica Plain offers a unique and appealing living experience. Whether exploring its green spaces, enjoying its diverse culinary scene, or participating in its vibrant cultural life, Jamaica Plain provides a welcoming and dynamic environment for all.

South Boston (Southie)

South Boston, affectionately known as "Southie," is a dynamic neighborhood located just south and east of downtown Boston. Historically a working-class Irish-American enclave, South Boston has undergone significant transformation in recent years, blending its rich cultural heritage with modern development and vibrant urban living.

South Boston's waterfront, particularly along the South Boston Seaport, has seen extensive redevelopment, transforming the area into a bustling hub of activity. The Harborwalk, a public walkway that stretches along the waterfront, offers scenic views of Boston Harbor and connects visitors to a variety of parks, beaches, and cultural attractions. Castle Island, home to Fort Independence, is a popular destination for walking, picnicking, and enjoying the harbor views.

The neighborhood's commercial corridors, such as Broadway and East and West Broadway, are lined with a diverse array of shops, restaurants, and bars. From traditional Irish pubs like The Seapoint Bar to trendy eateries and cafes, South Boston offers a vibrant dining and nightlife scene that caters to both long-time residents and newcomers.

South Boston's housing landscape is a mix of historic triple-decker homes, new luxury condos, and modern apartment complexes. This blend of old and new reflects the neighborhood's evolution while maintaining its distinctive character. The neighborhood's tight-knit community and strong local pride are evident in the numerous community events and parades, such as the famous St. Patrick's Day Parade, which draws large crowds each year.

The South Boston waterfront is also home to several significant cultural institutions, including the Institute of Contemporary Art (ICA), which features cutting-edge exhibitions and performances, and the Boston Convention and Exhibition Center, which hosts a variety of large-scale events and conferences.

South Boston's parks and recreational facilities provide ample opportunities for outdoor activities. Moakley Park, Marine Park, and the South Boston Maritime Park offer green spaces for sports, relaxation, and community gatherings.

With its mix of historic charm, modern amenities, and a strong sense of community, South Boston offers a unique and appealing living experience. Whether exploring its waterfront, enjoying its culinary and cultural offerings, or participating in its vibrant community life, South Boston provides a dynamic and welcoming environment for all.

Allston-Brighton

Allston-Brighton is a bustling and diverse neighborhood located in the western part of Boston, known for its vibrant student population, eclectic cultural scene, and a mix of residential and commercial areas. The neighborhood is home to a significant number of college students and young professionals, largely due to its proximity to Boston University, Boston College, and Harvard University.

Allston, often referred to as "Rock City," is known for its lively music scene, with numerous live music venues and bars hosting local and touring bands. The area's cultural diversity is reflected in its wide array of restaurants and eateries, offering everything from Korean barbecue and sushi to Middle Eastern falafel and classic American diners. Harvard Avenue and Brighton Avenue are the main commercial thoroughfares in Allston, lined with eclectic shops, cafes, and nightlife options.

Brighton, which borders Allston to the west, has a more residential feel, with tree-lined streets and a mix of apartment buildings, single-family homes, and condominiums. Brighton Center serves as the neighborhood's commercial hub, offering a variety of shops, restaurants, and services catering to the local community.

One of the notable green spaces in Allston-Brighton is the Charles River Reservation, a scenic area along the Charles River that offers walking and biking paths, rowing, and other recreational activities. The Chestnut Hill Reservoir, located in Brighton, is another popular spot for jogging, walking, and enjoying the outdoors.

Allston-Brighton is well-connected to the rest of Boston by public transportation, with several MBTA Green Line stops and bus routes providing easy access to downtown and other neighborhoods. This accessibility, combined with the area's vibrant atmosphere and diverse population, makes it a popular place to live for students, young professionals, and families alike.

Whether exploring its diverse dining options, enjoying a live music performance, or taking a leisurely stroll along the Charles River, Allston-Brighton offers a dynamic and engaging urban experience. Its blend of cultural vibrancy, educational institutions, and residential charm makes it a distinctive and appealing part of Boston.

Roslindale

Roslindale, often affectionately called "Rozzie" by locals, is a charming and diverse neighborhood located in the southwestern part of Boston. Known for its suburban feel within the city, Roslindale offers a mix of residential streets, bustling commercial areas, and lush green spaces that appeal to families, young professionals, and retirees alike.

Roslindale Village, the neighborhood's main commercial district, serves as the heart of the community. The village is lined with a variety of independent shops, cafes, restaurants, and services, giving it a small-town atmosphere. The Roslindale Village Farmers Market, held seasonally in Adams Park, is one of the largest and most popular farmers markets in Boston, attracting residents from across the city with its fresh produce, artisanal goods, and live entertainment.

One of Roslindale's most notable features is the Arnold Arboretum, a 281-acre botanical garden and part of the Emerald Necklace conservancy.

Managed by Harvard University, the Arboretum offers a peaceful retreat with its beautifully landscaped grounds, extensive plant collections, and miles of walking trails. It is a beloved destination for nature lovers, providing a stunning backdrop for outdoor activities and educational programs.

The neighborhood's residential areas are characterized by tree-lined streets, well-maintained single-family homes, and multi-family houses, reflecting its history as a commuter suburb. The community is known for its active neighborhood associations and strong sense of local pride, fostering a welcoming and inclusive environment.

Public transportation options, including the MBTA's Orange Line and commuter rail services, make Roslindale easily accessible from downtown Boston and other parts of the city. This convenient connectivity, combined with the neighborhood's green spaces and vibrant local businesses, makes Roslindale an attractive place to live.

Roslindale's cultural diversity is evident in its array of dining options, which range from traditional American fare to international cuisines, including Italian, Middle Eastern, and Caribbean. This culinary variety, along with the neighborhood's community events and festivals, contributes to its lively and inclusive atmosphere.

With its blend of suburban tranquility, vibrant community life, and proximity to downtown Boston, Roslindale offers a unique and appealing living experience. Whether enjoying the natural beauty of the Arnold Arboretum, shopping in Roslindale Village, or participating in local events, residents and visitors alike are drawn to the neighborhood's charm and sense of community.

Chinatown

Boston's Chinatown is a bustling and culturally rich neighborhood located in the heart of downtown Boston. As the third-largest Chinatown in the United States, it serves as a vibrant center for the city's Chinese community and offers a unique blend of cultural traditions, culinary delights, and historical significance.

Chinatown's streets are lined with a diverse array of shops, markets, and restaurants, offering everything from traditional Chinese herbal medicine and fresh produce to dim sum and bubble tea. The neighborhood's culinary scene is a major draw, with a plethora of dining options that reflect the rich tapestry of Chinese cuisine, including Cantonese, Sichuan, and Taiwanese dishes. Popular establishments like Hei La Moon, Gourmet Dumpling House, and Shojo Boston are well-known for their authentic flavors and bustling atmospheres.

One of the neighborhood's most iconic landmarks is the Chinatown Gate, located at the intersection of Beach Street and Surface Road. The gate, adorned with traditional Chinese architectural elements and symbols, serves as a welcoming entrance to the neighborhood and a symbol of its cultural heritage.

Chinatown is also home to several cultural and community organizations, such as the Chinese Consolidated Benevolent Association and the Boston Chinatown Neighborhood Center, which provide social services, cultural programs, and advocacy for the community. These organizations play a crucial role in preserving and promoting the neighborhood's cultural identity and supporting its residents.

The Rose Kennedy Greenway, a linear park that runs through Chinatown, offers a green oasis amidst the urban environment. The Greenway hosts various public art installations, cultural events, and community activities, providing a space for relaxation and recreation. The Chinatown Park section of the Greenway features traditional Chinese landscaping elements, including a serpentine walkway, bamboo groves, and a pagoda.

Chinatown's strategic location near major Boston landmarks such as the Theater District, Downtown Crossing, and South Station makes it easily accessible and a popular destination for both locals and tourists. The neighborhood's vibrant atmosphere, rich cultural heritage, and culinary diversity make it a unique and dynamic part of the city.

Whether exploring its bustling streets, enjoying a delicious meal, or participating in cultural events, visitors to Boston's Chinatown are sure to experience the neighborhood's distinctive charm and vitality. Its blend of tradition and modernity, along with its strong sense of community, make Chinatown an essential and enduring part of Boston's urban fabric.

Food and Dining

Iconic Boston Foods

Boston is famous for its iconic foods, each deeply embedded in the city's culinary fabric and cultural identity. Clam chowder, lobster rolls, and baked beans are not just foods in Boston—they are institutions, beloved by locals and tourists alike. Each of these quintessential Boston eats has its own unique history and places to find the best versions in the city.

Clam Chowder

Boston's clam chowder is world-renowned, known for its creamy texture and hearty ingredients. This rich, comforting soup features clams, potatoes, onions, and celery, all brought together in a velvety cream base.

Clam chowder has been a staple of New England cuisine since the 18th century, with Boston playing a significant role in popularizing this dish. Traditionally served with oyster crackers, Boston clam chowder is a must-try for anyone visiting the city.

Some of the most famous places to enjoy clam chowder in Boston include:

- **Union Oyster House:** The oldest continuously operating restaurant in the United States, serving classic New England clam chowder.
- **Legal Sea Foods:** A Boston institution known for its award-winning clam chowder.
- **Boston Chowda Co.:** Located in Quincy Market, it offers a delicious, traditional clam chowder experience.

Lobster Rolls

The lobster roll is another culinary icon of Boston, characterized by its generous portions of fresh lobster meat served in a toasted, buttery roll.

This dish highlights the region's rich maritime heritage and abundance of fresh seafood.

Boston's lobster rolls come in two main styles: the classic New England style with chilled lobster salad mixed with mayonnaise, and the Connecticut style, served warm with melted butter. Both versions are equally beloved by locals and visitors alike.

Some of the most celebrated places to enjoy lobster rolls in Boston include:

- **Neptune Oyster:** Located in the North End, known for its exceptional warm lobster roll.
- **James Hook & Co.:** A waterfront favorite offering a traditional New England-style lobster roll.
- **Row 34:** A popular spot in the Seaport District, known for its fresh seafood and outstanding lobster rolls.

Baked Beans

Boston baked beans are a historic staple, giving the city its nickname, "Beantown." This dish consists of navy beans slow-cooked with molasses, brown sugar, and salt pork, resulting in a rich, sweet flavor.

Baked beans have been a part of Boston's culinary tradition since colonial times, often served as a hearty accompaniment to other New England fare. The use of molasses in the recipe reflects Boston's historical ties to the molasses trade.

Some iconic spots to try Boston baked beans include:

- **Durgin-Park:** A historic restaurant in Faneuil Hall serving traditional New England cuisine, including famous baked beans.
- **The Warren Tavern:** One of the oldest taverns in America, located in Charlestown, offering classic Boston baked beans.
- **Union Oyster House:** Alongside their clam chowder, they also serve a delicious version of Boston baked beans.

Each of these iconic foods—clam chowder, lobster rolls, and baked beans—represents a slice of Boston's rich culinary history. Sampling these treats is not just about enjoying great food; it's about experiencing a piece of the city's vibrant culture and traditions.

Fine Dining

Boston is home to some of the region's most renowned fine dining establishments, offering exquisite culinary experiences that attract food enthusiasts from around the globe. The city's fine dining scene is characterized by its diversity, innovation, and the presence of several award-winning restaurants.

Award-Winning Restaurants

Boston boasts a number of prestigious restaurants, representing a wide array of cuisines and styles. These establishments are known for their meticulous attention to detail, exceptional service, and the use of the finest ingredients.

- **No. 9 Park:** Located in the historic Beacon Hill, No. 9 Park by Chef Barbara Lynch offers an intimate dining experience with a menu inspired by French and Italian cuisine. Known for its sophisticated ambiance and meticulously crafted dishes, it's a must-visit for fine dining aficionados.
- **Ostra:** A contemporary Mediterranean seafood restaurant, Ostra is celebrated for its elegant atmosphere and exceptional seafood dishes. Chef Jamie Mammano's attention to detail and innovative approach to Mediterranean cuisine have earned Ostra numerous accolades.
- **Menton:** Another gem by Chef Barbara Lynch, Menton combines French and Italian influences to create a unique fine dining experience. Located in the Fort Point neighborhood, it has received multiple awards for its exquisite tasting menus and impeccable service.

Internationally Inspired Fine Dining

Boston's fine dining scene also includes a variety of internationally inspired restaurants that bring global flavors to the city.

- **Uni:** This Japanese-inspired restaurant by Chef Tony Messina and Chef Ken Oringer offers an innovative take on sushi and

sashimi. Uni's omakase experience, featuring fresh, high-quality ingredients, has made it one of the best sushi restaurants in Boston.
- **Deuxave:** Located in the Back Bay, Deuxave by Chef Chris Coombs offers French-inspired cuisine with a contemporary twist. The elegant setting and inventive dishes make it a favorite among fine dining enthusiasts.
- **Mistral:** Situated in the South End, Mistral features a menu that blends French and Mediterranean influences. Chef Jamie Mammano's innovative dishes and the sophisticated atmosphere have earned Mistral a reputation as one of Boston's premier dining destinations.

These establishments represent the pinnacle of Boston's culinary scene, offering unique and memorable dining experiences that showcase the city's commitment to excellence and innovation in the culinary arts. Whether you're seeking traditional French cuisine, contemporary Mediterranean dishes, or innovative sushi, Boston's fine dining scene offers something for every discerning palate.

Casual Eateries

Boston's casual eateries offer a relaxed dining experience without compromising on quality. From neighborhood bistros to trendy cafes, these establishments provide a diverse range of delicious and affordable options.

Neighborhood Favorites

Casual eateries in Boston are often neighborhood institutions, beloved by locals for their cozy ambiance and consistently good food.
- **The Friendly Toast:** With locations in Back Bay and Cambridge, The Friendly Toast is known for its eclectic decor and extensive menu of comfort food. Popular dishes include the breakfast burrito and the stuffed French toast.

- **Santarpio's Pizza:** This East Boston hotspot is famous for its wood-fired pizzas and laid-back vibe. The menu also features a variety of grilled meats and classic Italian-American dishes.
- **Orinoco:** A charming Venezuelan bistro in the South End, Orinoco offers a menu of simple yet delicious dishes like arepas, empanadas, and pabellón criollo. Its intimate setting makes it perfect for brunch or a casual dinner.

Trendy Cafes and Diners

Boston is also home to a plethora of trendy cafes and diners that serve up everything from classic American fare to innovative brunch dishes.

- **Tatte Bakery & Cafe:** With several locations around the city, Tatte is known for its Mediterranean-inspired menu, including shakshuka, avocado toast, and a variety of pastries. The stylish decor and cozy atmosphere make it a favorite among locals.
- **The Paramount:** Located on Charles Street in Beacon Hill, The Paramount is a popular diner known for its hearty breakfast and lunch options, including omelets, pancakes, and sandwiches. Its bustling, casual vibe adds to its charm.
- **Mike's City Diner:** Famous for its generous portions and classic diner fare, this South End institution draws crowds for its all-day breakfast and comfort food offerings. The corned beef hash and turkey dinners are standout dishes.

Each of these casual eateries—neighborhood favorites and trendy cafes alike—offers a slice of Boston's rich culinary scene. Sampling these spots provides not just great food but also a taste of the city's vibrant culture and community spirit.

Street Food and Food Trucks

Boston's street food and food truck scene is vibrant and diverse, offering a quick and delicious way to sample a wide range of cuisines. From classic Boston treats to gourmet food trucks, these mobile eateries are an integral part of the city's culinary landscape.

Classic Street Food

The city's classic street food vendors have become iconic symbols of Boston's fast-paced lifestyle. In addition to the already mentioned classic treats, street carts in the city will offer:

- **Pretzels:** Soft pretzels, often sold from carts on busy street corners, are a popular snack. These warm, salty treats are perfect for a quick bite on the go.
- **Italian Sausages:** Boston's Italian heritage is celebrated with street vendors selling delicious Italian sausages with peppers and onions, often found around sporting events and festivals.

Gourmet Food Trucks

The city's food truck scene has exploded in recent years, with gourmet trucks offering inventive and high-quality dishes from around the world.

- **Bon Me:** This food truck fuses Vietnamese flavors with contemporary street food, serving up delicious dishes like bánh mì sandwiches, rice bowls, and noodle salads.
- **Roxy's Grilled Cheese:** Known for its creative grilled cheese sandwiches and comfort food, Roxy's offers items like the Mighty Rib Melt and truffle fries.
- **The Cookie Monstah:** A popular dessert food truck, The Cookie Monstah offers a variety of freshly baked cookies and ice cream sandwiches, perfect for a sweet treat on the go.

Pop-Up Markets

In addition to individual food trucks, Boston hosts several pop-up markets where multiple vendors gather to offer a variety of street food options.

- **SoWa Open Market:** Held on Sundays from May through October, the SoWa Open Market features a rotating selection of food trucks, offering everything from gourmet tacos to artisanal ice cream. The market also includes local arts and crafts vendors.
- **Greenway Food Trucks:** Located along the Rose Kennedy Greenway, this food truck festival runs from April to October,

featuring a variety of trucks offering diverse and delicious options for lunch or dinner.

Whether you're craving a quick snack or a gourmet meal on the go, Boston's street food and food truck scene has something to satisfy every palate. These mobile eateries offer a convenient and delicious way to experience the city's diverse culinary offerings.

Ethnic Cuisine

Boston is a city with a rich tapestry of ethnic cuisines, reflecting its diverse neighborhoods and the legacy of immigrants who have made the city their home. The North End, Chinatown, and Allston are three of the most vibrant areas where visitors can indulge in authentic and delicious foods from around the world.

North End

The North End, located in downtown Boston, is a historic neighborhood that celebrates the legacy of Italian immigrants who settled in the city in the late 19th and early 20th centuries. Known as Boston's "Little Italy," the area retains its charming, old-world ambiance and remains a culinary haven for lovers of Italian cuisine.

Hanover Street, the heart of the North End, is lined with Italian restaurants, cafes, and bakeries that serve classic dishes such as pasta, pizza, and cannoli. Notable establishments include Regina Pizzeria, recognized as one of Boston's oldest and best pizzerias, where visitors can savor a slice of history along with their pie. For a sweet treat, Mike's Pastry, founded in 1946, offers a delightful selection of Italian pastries, including their famous cannoli.

The neighborhood is also famous for its annual Feast of Saint Anthony, a street festival held in August that celebrates the patron saint of lost things. The festival features parades, live music, food stalls, and religious processions, attracting visitors from around the world. During the feast, Hanover Street transforms into a lively celebration of Italian culture and cuisine, with vendors selling sausage and peppers, arancini, and other Italian street foods.

Chinatown

Chinatown, located in downtown Boston, is one of the largest and oldest Chinatowns in the United States. Established by Chinese immigrants in the mid-19th century, the neighborhood is a bustling enclave that offers a wide array of authentic Chinese cuisine.

Chinatown's streets are filled with markets, bakeries, and restaurants that showcase the diverse flavors of China. Dim sum, a traditional Cantonese meal of small plates, is a popular choice, with restaurants like Hei La Moon and China Pearl offering a variety of dumplings, buns, and other delicacies served from rolling carts. For a more casual bite, Gourmet Dumpling House is famous for its soup dumplings, a must-try for any visitor.

In addition to Cantonese cuisine, Chinatown also offers dishes from other regions of China. Spicy Sichuan cuisine can be found at restaurants like Clay Pot Cafe, while Penang serves dishes inspired by the flavors of Malaysia, including hand-pulled noodles and spicy lamb burgers.

Chinatown's vibrant food scene is complemented by its lively street markets, where vendors sell fresh produce, seafood, and exotic ingredients. These markets provide a glimpse into the neighborhood's rich culinary traditions and are a must-visit for any food enthusiast.

Food Markets

Boston is renowned for its diverse culinary landscape, and its food markets are some of the best places to experience this gastronomic variety. Among these, Quincy Market and the Boston Public Market stand out as must-visit destinations for food lovers seeking a wide array of flavors and culinary delights.

Quincy Market

Located in the heart of downtown Boston, Quincy Market is one of the city's most iconic indoor food markets. Part of the historic Faneuil Hall Marketplace, Quincy Market retains much of its historic charm with its beautiful Greek Revival architecture, cobblestone paths, and bustling atmosphere.

Quincy Market is a food lover's paradise, offering an eclectic mix of vendors that cater to a wide range of tastes and preferences. Visitors can find everything from classic New England clam chowder and lobster rolls to international fare like Greek gyros and Italian cannoli. Popular vendors include Boston Chowda Co., known for its creamy clam chowder and lobster bisque, and North End Bakery, famous for its pastries and cannoli.

In addition to its food stalls, Quincy Market features several sit-down restaurants where visitors can enjoy a full meal. Salty Dog Seafood Grille & Bar offers a menu focused on fresh seafood, while Cheers provides a classic American dining experience reminiscent of the famous TV show. The market also houses retail shops selling souvenirs, specialty foods, and unique gifts, making it a one-stop destination for both culinary delights and shopping.

Boston Public Market

The Boston Public Market, located at 100 Hanover Street, is an indoor market that showcases the best of New England's local produce and artisanal foods. Open year-round, the market is committed to providing fresh, locally sourced food from Massachusetts and the surrounding states.

The Boston Public Market features over 30 vendors offering a wide variety of products, including fresh fruits and vegetables, dairy products, meats, seafood, baked goods, and specialty foods. Notable vendors include Red's Best, known for its sustainably caught seafood, and Union Square Donuts, famous for its handcrafted donuts in unique flavors.

One of the highlights of the Boston Public Market is its emphasis on local and sustainable foods. Visitors can enjoy everything from farm-fresh produce and grass-fed meats to artisanal cheeses and handcrafted chocolates. The market also offers cooking demonstrations, workshops, and events that promote local food education and sustainability.

SoWa Open Market

The SoWa Open Market, located in the South End, is an open-air market that operates seasonally, typically from May to October. The market features a diverse array of food trucks, local farmers, and artisanal vendors, creating a vibrant community atmosphere.

The SoWa Open Market is a great place to sample a wide variety of foods from some of Boston's best food trucks. Popular food trucks include Bon Me, known for its Vietnamese-inspired sandwiches and noodle bowls, and Roxy's Grilled Cheese, famous for its creative grilled cheese sandwiches and comfort food. In addition to the food trucks, the market also features local farmers selling fresh produce, flowers, and specialty foods.

The lively atmosphere of the SoWa Open Market, combined with its rotating selection of vendors, makes it a perfect spot for a leisurely weekend outing. The market also includes local artists and craftspeople selling handmade goods, adding to the unique and eclectic experience.

Both Quincy Market and the Boston Public Market offer unique and memorable culinary experiences, showcasing the best of Boston's vibrant food scene. Whether you're exploring the historic indoor market of Quincy or indulging in the local offerings at the Boston Public Market, these food markets are essential destinations for any food enthusiast visiting the city.

Made in the USA
Monee, IL
27 March 2025